the story
of the Boston
Massacre

Mary Kay Phelan
illustrated by Allan Eitzen

Thomas Y. Crowell Company • New York

Library of Congress Cataloging in Publication Data
Phelan, Mary Kay.
The story of the Boston Massacre.
Bibliography: p. Includes index.
SUMMARY: Describes the events preceding, during,
and following the Boston Massacre, an incident with far-
reaching political consequences that eventually led to
the Revolution.
1. Boston Massacre, 1770—Juvenile literature.
[1. Boston Massacre, 1770] I. Eitzen, Allan. II. Title.
E215.4.P45   1975   973.3′113   75-25961
ISBN 0-690-00716-7

1 2 3 4 5 6 7 8 9 10

especially for Doris and Jerry

whose fascination for history matches mine

other books by
Mary Kay Phelan:

The Burning of Washington: August 1814
Four Days in Philadelphia—1776
Midnight Alarm: The Story of Paul Revere's Ride
Mr. Lincoln's Inaugural Journey
Probing the Unknown: The Story of
Dr. Florence Sabin
The Story of the Boston Tea Party
The Story of the Great Chicago Fire, 1871

acknowledgments

Many years after the Boston Massacre occurred, John Adams wrote: "On that night the foundation of American independence was laid." Historians sometimes refer to it as the first battle of the American Revolution, although open conflict did not begin for another five years. Nevertheless, the political effects of the massacre were far-reaching; the colonists began stiffening in their resistance toward arbitrary rule by Great Britain—a resistance that eventually culminated in the adoption of the Declaration of Independence on July 4, 1776.

In this recounting of the story of the Boston Massacre, all quotations are taken from original sources. No conversation is fictionized. Diaries, journals, Boston newspapers of 1768–1770, and contemporary accounts by participants have been invaluable. Of primary importance were John Adams' *Diary and Autobiography* (4 volumes), edited by L. H. Butterfield; the complete transcript of *Trial of the British Soldiers*; and *A Short Narrative of the Horrid Massacre in Boston . . . ,* originally printed by the town in 1770.

contents

the story
of the Boston
Massacre

secret conclave

Boston is seething with resentment in this early fall of 1768. All week long rumors have circulated through the crooked streets and winding lanes. King George III, it's reported, is sending troops to occupy the town. Some say there will be six thousand; others have heard that as many as ten thousand will be coming. *Ten thousand soldiers* stationed in a community of some sixteen thousand persons? Impossible! Yet the reports persist. Most people are infuriated at the very idea.

Less than a year ago, Royal customs officers arrived from London. They were authorized by the Crown to collect excessive duties on all imported goods. Even more insulting, they were to probe into the slightest trade violation.

Hatred of these officials has been widespread. There have been angry demonstrations against them, even minor riots. Several months ago, the customs men became frightened by the resistance among local citizenry. They demanded military protection of Parliament. Now, on this late afternoon of September 28, word is received that a number of armed frigates flying the British Union Jack have been sighted sailing toward Boston Harbor. They should be docking within a few days.

There are some who are pleased at the prospect of having soldiers stationed here. These people are known as Tories—wealthy, conservative, and proud to be a part of the powerful British Empire. They are friendly with Royal officials; they sympathize with George III and his efforts to obtain money for the Mother Country.

On the other hand, the group called Patriots (or Whigs) resist any infringement on their right to make their own laws, levy their own taxes. Freedom in this new land is a prized possession. For the most part, these people are well-educated—serious, responsible, and highly intelligent. They deplore the violence of the waterfront gangs, those mobs of young men and boys who frequently roam the streets and create destruction. The brawls, the "rumpuses," the burning in effigy of hated Crown officials—all are distasteful to the Patriots. They are reasonable citizens who prefer to use legal methods in opposing the King.

News of the British soldiers' impending arrival spreads quickly. Over at the Bunch of Grapes Tavern, Sam Adams is talking politics, something he does to whoever will listen. In defying the high-handed tactics of the British government, Adams is the unofficial leader of the Patriots' cause. As usual, a crowd has gathered around him. Intently he listens to all the arguments—never pressing too hard, never losing his temper. Yet he's gently persuasive in encouraging opposition to the Mother Country.

As the conversation continues, a sailor bursts into the taproom, shouting that the Royal ships are definitely on the way. He's seen them himself!

Sam Adams slips from the group, beckoning his fellow Patriot Will Molineux to follow him. Once outside the taproom, Adams whispers that the news is not unexpected. Still, their closest associates should be alerted. There are decisions to be made—this very night! Molineux nods in agreement and offers his home as a meeting place. The men part in haste, after Adams has promised to dispatch the necessary messages.

It is shortly before 7 P.M. when the Patriot leader emerges from his dilapidated wooden house on Purchase Street, the home where he has lived ever since he was born forty-seven years ago. Dressed in a shabby brown suit shiny from years of wear, Sam Adams tosses his worn red cloak carelessly around his shoulders as he hurries down the front steps. Turning up toward Molineux's house in the North End, Sam has a look of determination. His is a strong face. The brow is high and broad; from it sweeps back the thinning gray hair, now rumpled by the wind blowing in across the harbor. The steel-gray eyes have a grave expression. The nose is prominent; the thin lips, the firm chin point up the strength of character so evident in this Patriot.

Financially, Sam Adams has never been a success. After receiving his master's degree from Harvard College, he drifted from one job to another—failing at each. Even as Boston's tax collector he had troubles; he could never bring himself to demand money from the poor. Eventually he lost that position too. Though the small inheritance from his father is almost gone, Sam remains unconcerned. Someway, somehow, his wife Betsy will manage to feed and clothe the family. She always has!

For the past few years politics has been Sam Adams' only profession. His range of friends is wide: wealthy merchants and influential citizens, carpenters and shipwrights, laborers on the docks, workers from the ropewalks. He analyzes every regulation that Parliament imposes on the colonies and explains its significance to the people. Adams makes it his business to convince as many as possible that the British government must not be allowed to infringe on their liberties. In fact, he's often called the "watchdog of colonial rights."

Now, turning into Brattle Square from Cornhill Street, Sam recognizes the stout little man just ahead. It's his cousin, John Adams, who recently arrived from his native Braintree to practice law in Boston. The Patriot leader smiles. His message to meet at Molineux's tonight has been delivered, all right. Lengthening his stride, Sam soon catches up with the lawyer. In a hushed voice, he tells John that tonight's meeting is very important. Decisions must be made about how the British soldiers will be received in Boston.

John Adams is thirteen years younger than his cousin, and very different in temperament; nevertheless the two men have great respect for each other. The lawyer has firm convictions about the liberties, the privileges, of the colonists. Yet he inclines toward gradual change rather than any sudden upheaval. On the other hand, Cousin Sam is far more liberal, and many of his judgments are based on emotion rather than logic. Still, John admires the Patriot leader's persuasiveness, his ability to recruit people to their cause.

As the two approach the corner of Beacon and Mount Vernon Streets, Sam points out that their host, Will Molineux, has already shuttered the tiny paned windows of his home. "Splendid!" says Sam. No one understands better than Molineux the need for secrecy tonight. The merchant allied himself with the Patriots several years ago. Heavy taxes imposed by Parliament have ruined his hardware business. Now thoroughly angered, Molineux is ready to take drastic steps for revenge.

In answer to Sam Adams' knock, Molineux inches open the front door. Silently he motions the two men to step inside the shadowy hallway. The darkness is a precautionary measure, the merchant explains; in fact, he's lighted only one candle in the front parlor. No outsider must know who is here tonight. The Adamses nod in agreement.

Within a few minutes, Dr. Joseph Warren and Paul Revere join the gathering. The two men are a study in contrasts; yet the friendship that exists between them

is strong. Twenty-nine-year-old Joseph Warren was graduated from Harvard College and served his medical apprenticeship under Dr. James Lloyd. Blond in appearance, with kindly blue eyes and a gentle manner, he is the town's most successful physician. In 1763 when a widespread smallpox epidemic broke out, Warren took the lead in insisting on inoculation. Despite dissension over such an unheard-of procedure, he was able to save many lives. Ever since coming to Boston, the physician has been an ardent follower of Sam Adams and his beliefs.

Paul Revere, on the other hand, is a burly little person with a swarthy complexion and dark eyes. Though he has had little formal schooling, Revere has many talents. A silversmith by trade, his blunt, capable hands fashion the most beautiful silver pieces in Boston. He's taught himself to make copper-plate engravings. The pictures he prints are political cartoons that amuse the people who buy them. Just a few months ago, Revere learned the art of making false teeth, carving them from the ivory of hippopotamus tusks. Fearless in his actions, Paul is greatly admired by his fellow Patriots for the courage that he shows in defying the Mother Country. They have nicknamed him "Bold Revere."

The last one to arrive for tonight's meeting is

lawyer Josiah Quincy, Jr. Youngest of the group (he's only twenty-six), Quincy is a frail-looking man with a cast in one eye. His thin face is heavily lined—evidence of the tuberculosis that racks his body. Aware that he does not have many years to live, Josiah is determined to crowd as much as possible into his limited time span. In addition to a large law practice, he devotes endless hours to the Patriots' cause—speaking at mass meetings and writing articles for the *Boston Gazette*, which he signs "Mentor" or "The Old Man."

The problems these six men are discussing tonight began after the French and Indian War ended five years ago. Although the victorious British had driven the French out of Canada, the seven-year conflict had been an expensive business. Parliament was faced with overwhelming debts and very little revenue with which to meet them. Prime Minister George Grenville suggested the idea of taxing the colonists. After all, he said, they were protected by the British army and navy; it was only fair for them to pay part of the expenses of defense. Parliament agreed. But serious differences of opinion soon developed between England and her colonies.

For many years the colonists had conducted their own affairs without interference from the Mother Country. Suddenly to be required to pay taxes levied by a government three thousand miles away was unthinkable. Sam Adams protested: "If taxes are laid upon us in any shape without our having a legal representation where they are laid, are we not reduced from the character of free subjects to the miserable state of tributary slaves?" King George ignored all colonial dissent.

The Sugar Act, passed by Parliament in 1764, placed a duty on molasses, sugar, and wines imported from places outside the British Empire. Boston merchants, shipowners, and distillers of rum were angered by the new tax. But it was the Stamp Act, imposed the following year, that thoroughly aroused the citizenry.

This act provided that taxes be levied on newspapers, advertisements, playing cards, college diplomas, and all legal documents, such as property deeds, notes and bonds, wills, ships' clearance papers. (A Royal stamp was required to show that the tax had been paid; thus the name Stamp Act.) Benjamin Edes, editor of the *Boston Gazette,* was enraged. He called it an assault on the freedom of the press and removed the King's insignia from the front page of his paper, replacing it with a drawing of a skull and crossbones.

Resentment increased. The Patriots encouraged everyone to reject the stamps. Colonial merchants signed "Non-Importation Agreements," promising not to buy or import any British goods. Violence became more frequent in Boston. Stamps were burned in the streets; offices of the stamp collectors were destroyed; homes of Royal officials were attacked.

Parliament was shocked by the hostility that the Stamp Act had aroused. In addition to the general dismay over colonial demonstrations, British merchants were feeling the impact of the Non-Importation Agreements. Trade had practically ceased between England and the colonies. Under heavy pressure, Parliament repealed the Stamp Act on March 18, 1766.

The news brought great rejoicing in Boston. But this exuberant spirit was short-lived. Just last year, in 1767, Charles Townshend, Chancellor of the Exchequer, demanded that Parliament pass the Townshend Acts, designed to increase revenue. These placed import duties on tea, lead, glass, and pigments for paint. In addition, a law was enacted to establish a Royal Board of Customs Commissioners, headquartered in Boston and staffed by agents appointed in England. These customs officers arrived last November, armed with written statements (called "Writs of Assistance") that gave them legal authority to search a man's ship, his business establishment, even his home. It is because of the violent opposition these Royal officers have experienced that troops are now coming to Boston to protect them.

Tonight, the men gathered at Will Molineux's home consider every angle of this latest insult. The meeting is a stormy one. Hot-tempered Molineux wants to offer armed resistance. He reminds the group that last July local authorities ordered the town's arms to be taken out of the attic in Faneuil Hall, where town meetings are held. The four hundred muskets were cleaned and now are stacked on the main floor of the building. These, he says, could be distributed secretly to sympathetic citizens.

Dr. Warren and Paul Revere are undecided about armed resistance, but Sam Adams negates any such proposal. Every legal means possible must be explored in dealing with Parliament before any drastic measures are taken. Lawyers John Adams and Josiah Quincy agree.

Patiently, Sam points out that arming the town's population could produce an undesirable explosion. Rather, he suggests, the Patriots should adopt a policy of "dignified non-cooperation." Molineux continues to argue for resistance by force. Eventually, however, he is persuaded to the more moderate course of action.

Glancing at his pocket watch, John Adams suggests that it's getting late. To avoid undue suspicion about tonight's meeting, they should all be home before the

9 P.M. curfew. After shaking hands, the men steal out a side door into the darkened street. Footsteps echo on the cobblestones as the Patriots go their separate ways. They cannot help but wonder how the town will react to the presence of British troops. Is there trouble brewing for the future?

invasion of redcoats

september 29–november 10, 1768

Over at Province House, official residence of the Royal governor, Francis Bernard paces the floor of his study in agitation. The British troops will be docking within a few days. But the problem of where to house the men is still not solved.

The Patriots like to describe Bernard as "a roast-beef of a man," with influential connections. Commissioned by King George III, the governor came to Boston eight years ago. His lack of experience soon became evident; his reign has not been a popular one. Indecisive and somewhat slow-witted, Francis Bernard has consistently mishandled the affairs of the Massachusetts Bay Colony.

Because the King of England wishes to maintain a semblance of control over the colony, he appoints the governor, the lieutenant governor, and the secretary of the province—loyal Tories all. The law-making body is composed of two houses: the Council, or upper house, and the Assembly, or lower house. Membership in the Assembly is comprised of a representative from each town in the colony, elected by the people in a town meeting. This more liberal group then selects those who will make up the twenty-eight-member Council. However, the governor has veto power over any choice. Francis Bernard has used that veto often in his attempt to find Council members who will be sympathetic to Great Britain.

Yesterday afternoon, word reached Province House that six ships of the British flotilla were anchored in Nantasket Roads. The governor left immediately by boat for Castle William, the fortress located on an island three miles down the harbor. It was important, he felt, to establish a good relationship with Lieutenant Colonel William Dalrymple, who commands the troops sent to Boston by Parliament.

After a brief exchange of greetings, Dalrymple asked what provisions had been made for housing his men. Bernard launched into a tedious description of his troubles with the councilmen—they had been most uncooperative . . . they had opposed every move he made. At last the governor came to the point: no quarters were available. Dalrymple was furious, accusing Bernard of failing to exercise his legal power. It was evident to the commander that he could expect little assistance from the civil administration.

Now, on this Wednesday morning, September 29, the harassed governor is calling his Council together. When the men arrive, he takes them by boat out to Castle William, intent on proving his helpless position to the lieutenant colonel.

Dalrymple remains firm. He reminds the councilmen of the Quartering Act, which Parliament passed three years ago—the act requiring colonial authorities to provide barracks and supplies for British troops stationed in America. The commander explains he has orders to quarter his regiments in Boston, and he prefers barracks where the officers can keep the soldiers under strict supervision. With a half-smile, Dalrymple adds that he hopes he is going to be among friends.

The plea for good will is disregarded. A noisy dispute follows. There's no need to bring the troops into town, the councilmen insist. Legally, the fortress is a part of Boston; Dalrymple can station the soldiers there and still comply with the King's orders.

In a voice filled with contempt, the commanding officer points out that he does not evade responsibility. He does not question orders; he obeys them. Therefore he intends to march his men into town. If barracks are not provided, Dalrymple will not be responsible for the conduct of his troops.

Wrangling between the governor and his Council continues for several hours. Eventually the members pass a resolution "to make no Provision for the Troops in Boston, on any Pretense," and the meeting breaks up.

As the men stalk out of Castle William, Dalrymple takes Bernard aside. Why is he so spineless? the officer wants to know. Can't he exert his authority? The governor throws up his hands. On the question of providing housing he is powerless. Furthermore, he intends to write to the Earl of Hillsborough, Secretary of State for the Colonies, to demand that all future councilmen be appointed by the Crown. The commander turns away in disgust.

All day Thursday, an uneasy silence hovers over the town. The people watch—and wait. Early Friday morning, there's a thunderous boom of guns from Castle William saluting the twelve transports and schooners as they begin moving into the harbor. After each vessel has dropped anchor alongside the dock, a

spring is attached to her cable. Thus the ship can be swung around easily, with the guns ready to fire. Paul Revere reports to his friend Dr. Warren that the men-of-war are maneuvering "as for a regular siege."

Precisely at noon on Friday, October 1, the 14th and 29th Regiments, accompanied by a train of artillery, come ashore at Long Wharf. The soldiers take parade formation on the dock. Drums beat a steady tattoo; shrill fifes set the pace for marching feet, as the long lines begin moving up King Street.

No one can deny that the British troops present a colorful appearance—the soldiers in their stiff red coats, the drummers (many of them black) wearing bright yellow jackets. The tallest men in the regiments, the grenadiers, have high bearskin caps. On the front of each cap is the House of Hanover's white horse badge and motto: *Nec aspera terrent* ("They fear no difficulty"). Officers can be identified by the crimson sash worn over their shoulders and the crescent-shaped silver breastplate across their chests.

Silent crowds line the streets to watch the soldiers parade by. The drawn swords of the officers give them the appearance of troops taking possession of a conquered town. The people are stunned. Governor Bernard has proclaimed that the British are here "to rescue the Government from the hands of a trained mob and to restore the activity of the Civil Power." That statement does nothing to reassure the citizenry. Still, not one word of protest is uttered this afternoon. Sam Adams' plea for "dignified non-cooperation" from his fellow townsmen seems to have been heeded.

Past the Custom House, past the Town House, the troops march, turning into Queen Street and then left on Treamount. By 4 P.M. both regiments are lined up on Boston Common. The cows usually pastured here have scattered in haste as the soldiers approached.

Meanwhile, Lieutenant Colonel Dalrymple, who left his men immediately after the ships docked, is searching frantically for some place to house them. Yesterday Governor Bernard sent word to Castle William that Manufactory House might be available. The commander hurries over to make the necessary arrangements.

About fifty years ago, a group of emigrants from Londonderry, Ireland, settled in Boston. They brought with them both the tools and the skill for manufacturing linen. Until that time colonial women had been wearing coarse homespun—and disliking it. Everyone wanted to learn how to make the new fabric. Town officials approved and voted to establish a spinning school. The huge Manufactory House was built, and it soon overflowed with women and their wheels; spinning became the rage. But after three years the fad died out. The various rooms in the house are now rented to private families.

Dalrymple is confounded by the tenants' reaction to his request. British soldiers in their homes? Never! They refuse to budge. Dalrymple next approaches the town officials; they are indifferent. Housing unwanted soldiers is no concern of theirs, they tell the distracted commander.

Aware that the 29th Regiment is carrying tents and field equipment, the lieutenant colonel hastens over to the Common. He calls his officers together and admits that his search for quarters has been futile. Instruct the men of the 29th to pitch their tents on the Common, he orders. They'll have to camp out of doors until more permanent quarters can be found. Then he leads the troops of the 14th down to Faneuil Hall. There the soldiers stand at parade rest for two hours while their commander again argues with town officials. Eventually he manages to pry one of the doors open, and beds down his men in the Hall. They are much too crowded, but at least it's a place to rest for the night. Not only has Dalrymple taken over Boston's town meeting place, he has also secured the four hundred town muskets.

Shortly after 8 P.M., John Adams rides into town.

He has been out on the circuit trying law cases in the county courts. The sight of the redcoats swarming through the streets astounds the lawyer. To his diary he confides: "Their very appearance in Boston was a strong proof to me that the determination of Great Britain to subjugate us was too deep and inveterate ever to be altered by us."

Early Sunday morning, Governor Bernard gets in touch with Lieutenant Colonel Dalrymple. The entire Town House (where the legislative body meets) will be available for the men of the 14th Regiment, Bernard reports. Very soon the overflow from Faneuil Hall is settled in the Town House. Sentinels are stationed at the steps, and British cannon placed across the street point directly at the legislature's doors. Civilians on their way to church this morning are distressed and bewildered by the sight of the artillery.

Over in his little silversmith's shop at the head of Clark's Wharf, Paul Revere busies himself this afternoon with a copper-plate engraving of the troop landing. He intends to print pictures from the engraving—pictures that will record for posterity the arrival of the British men-of-war. In the scroll-like design below the scene, Revere inscribes the following:

> To the Earl of Hillsborough . . . this view of the only well-planned expedition formed for supporting ye

dignity of Britain in chastising the insolence of America, is humbly dedicated.

As the October days grow shorter, Governor Bernard is still unable to solve the housing problem. The men of the 14th cannot remain on the drafty floors of Faneuil Hall and the Town House indefinitely. Certainly no one could expect the 29th to camp out all winter on the windswept Common. Already the men are beginning to desert, slipping away at night into the surrounding countryside and not returning. The governor issues a proclamation offering a reward of ten guineas to the soldier "who should inform of anyone who should attempt to seduce him from the service." Bernard strongly suspects that these desertions are being encouraged by the Patriots.

By late in the month more than forty soldiers have left. Dalrymple decides that he must take drastic action. Private Richard Ames of the 14th has been caught in the act of deserting. He is court-martialed and sentenced to face a firing squad. Both regiments are lined up on the Common to watch; a general invitation is issued to any civilians who care to attend the execution.

Boston townspeople are not accustomed to the strict military discipline of the British. The execution of a soldier for desertion is a horrifying sight. Lesser infringements are often punished by ceremonial whippings on the Common—cruel and even sometimes fatal to the redcoats who have committed the misdemeanors.

By October 27, Dalrymple has managed to lease vacant warehouses, stores, and distilleries in the area around the Custom House. The soldiers move in, relieved to have permanent barracks. Most of the officers have rented rooms in private homes. The lieutenant colonel has found lodgings in Green's Lane. He dislikes the idea of not being nearer his troops, and repeats his former warning to the governor: unless the officers are quartered with the men, Dalrymple cannot be responsible for their actions.

More transports sail into Boston Harbor on November 10, bringing the 54th and 65th Regiments from Ireland. By contrast, this disembarkation is effected smoothly. Some of the men will be stationed at the fortress on Castle Island; Lieutenant Colonel Dalrymple has already found quarters for the others. Now there are four thousand redcoats here—one soldier for every four civilians. The town is swarming with Britishers—on the streets, in the stores, at the markets. Shopping for food becomes a nearly impossible task for Boston housewives; the officers are always there first, taking the best cuts of meat, the choicest fish.

Soldiers flaunting their power in a resentful town will not be tolerated indefinitely. Everyone knows that something is sure to happen. The question now is, "How soon?"

st. botolph's town in 1768

By New World standards, the community in which the British soldiers find themselves stationed is very old. The Puritans landed at Plymouth Rock in 1620. Ten years later, Governor John Winthrop brought his hardy band of settlers to this region that the Indians called Shawmut, or "Place Where Boats Land." But the town's eventual name has an interesting origin.

Centuries ago, sailors in Britain had only crude boats with which to battle a cruel ocean. A Saxon monk living in Lincolnshire spent his days praying for these sailors' safety. People called him the "Boat-Helper"—in their language, Bot-holph. After the monk died, he was made a saint. A church was built in his honor and a village grew up around it—a village called Saint Botolph's Town. Through the centuries the name changed to Bottleston, Buston, and finally Boston: Boston, Lincolnshire, England. Many of Winthrop's colonists had come from Saint Botolph's village. Homesick for familiar surroundings, they voted to name this new settlement Boston.

Like a giant fist jutting into the ocean, the peninsula on which the community is located is almost entirely surrounded by water. The narrow mile-long causeway, called Boston Neck, is the residents' only link with the mainland. Heavy tides washing over the Neck sometimes turn the town into an island.

When the British men-of-war sailed into the harbor recently, soldiers on the ships' decks first saw three large hills rising against the skyline. Later they learned their names: Fort Hill near the eastern shore, Copps Hill to the northeast, and Trimontaine in the northwest. Trimontaine is divided into three smaller hills: Mount Vernon, Pemberton, and Beacon. It is on Beacon Hill that the wealthy merchants have chosen to build their three-story mansions.

Spreading out below Beacon Hill is the fifty-acre Boston Common. The town purchased the land from William Blackstone in 1634, and Governor Winthrop decreed it to be "for common use as a cow pasture and training field." Here too is Frog Pond, where the early Puritans used to duck persons who disobeyed the Sabbath laws, or women who nagged their husbands.

All land traffic approaches from the south, along the desolate cart path on the Neck. On the right travelers see the Gallows, with its small clusters of stones marking the graves of executed criminals. Next is the brick Town Gate—double-arched, with two passage-ways. One is for pedestrians; the other for wagons, carriages, and horseback riders. Guards are stationed here around the clock, ready to challenge anyone who acts suspicious.

An unpaved pathway, Orange Street, leads in from the gate, but the town fans out quickly. On the west is Treamount Street, which eventually becomes Brattle Square. On the east are dozens of little lanes and alleys sloping down to the shore. There are few house numbers in Boston. Officials believe it is easier for strangers to find their way if the street names are changed at short intervals. Thus Orange Street be-comes Newbury, then Marlborough, and finally Corn-hill, terminating at King Street, the broadest and busiest thoroughfare in the main part of town.

Because King Street extends down to the shore and leads directly onto Long Wharf, this roadway teems

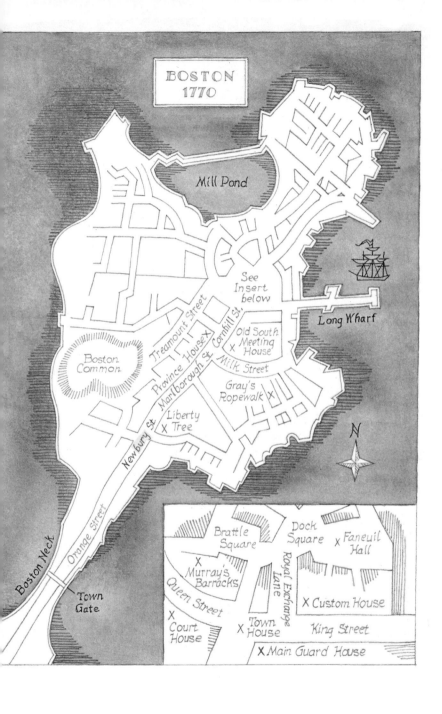

with noise all day long. There's a constant procession of two-wheeled carts, wagons, and drays lumbering out to the ships, or returning laden with cargo. The sound of horses' hooves striking the cobblestones, the frenzied shouts of drivers directing their animals, contribute to the confusion. Pedestrians walking along King Street are sometimes forced to leap to the safety of a shopkeeper's doorway to avoid an accident.

The wharf itself stretches out half a mile into the harbor, with a road in the center. On the north side are shops, sail lofts, warehouses, and the countingrooms of wealthy merchants. Along the open south side the world's largest ships dock, even at low tide. When Long Wharf was completed in 1710, it was considered an impressive feat of engineering; newcomers today still marvel at its construction.

At the head of King Street is the stately Town House, a two-story brick building whose clock tower can be seen for miles around. (On "rejoicing days," when Parliament has repealed an act undesirable to the colonists, the tower is lighted with hundreds of candles. Everyone celebrates!) The Town House serves a dual purpose. The lower floor is the Royal Exchange, where merchants gather every weekday at 1 P.M. to transact their business deals, just as Englishmen do in London.

The second floor is the seat of government for the province. Governor Bernard has an office here. The upper legislative body—the Council—meets in one chamber; the lower house—the Assembly—convenes in another. The most distinctive feature in the assemblymen's room is the large wooden codfish hanging from the ceiling. Some twenty years ago, John Rowe, an assemblyman, reminded his fellow legislators that the original settlers of Boston could not have survived without the cod. It was their first export, and for many years the only source of revenue from outside the province. Rowe suggested that a representation of the fish be hung "as a memorial of the importance of the Cod Fishery to the welfare of the nation." His motion was approved, and John Welch carved the fish from a single block of wood.

One block below the Town House, at the corner of Royal Exchange Lane, is the brick Custom House, presided over by Crown officials. Shipmasters come here to enter their vessels and pay the duties owed on their cargoes. All customs records are stored in this building, as well as whatever revenue cash has been collected.

The most imposing structure in town is Faneuil Hall, on nearby Dock Square. Thirty years ago, Peter Faneuil inherited a large fortune from his uncle and offered to build a marketplace for the people of Boston—a place where farmers could bring their produce, and housewives would come to purchase the fresh foods. The portrait painter John Smibert was the architect. After viewing the original drawings, Faneuil insisted that a public hall be added so the citizens could hold town meetings there.

Constructed of brick, the two-and-a-half-story building has a handsome cupola. British soldiers are amused by the grasshopper weathervane atop the cupola; it reminds them of the one on the Royal Exchange in London.

In the streets surrounding Dock Square are many small stores. They used to be filled with tempting arrays of goods from England—figured wallpapers, window glass, lusterware, and fine furniture. But now that most merchants have signed Non-Importation Agreements, the shelves are quite empty. Nevertheless the silversmiths, wigmakers, tailors, button molders, and cobblers do a thriving business. Young apprentices dressed in bulky leather aprons and full-cut leather breeches scurry through the streets to deliver the products of their masters.

Just recently several "cook shops" have been opened. Since few residences boast the luxury of an oven, housewives can now prepare food at home and take it to one of these shops to be roasted or baked.

Many prefer this to the old-fashioned way of cooking over an open fireplace, especially when the weather is hot.

Edging the eastern shoreline is a vast network of piers, wharves, shipyards, distilleries, and warehouses. The harbor bristles with vessels—broad-beamed sloops loaded with firewood from Maine, ketches that bring cargo from the West Indies, sailing schooners with treasures from the Iberian Peninsula and southern France: salt, wine, fruits, laces, and fine linens to delight the Yankee population. Nestled among the larger craft are the tiny fishing boats that come in with fresh codfish, haddock, and mackerel, so important to the housewives' meal planning.

At night the streets are very dark. Some home-owners hang lighted lanterns in their doorways, but for the most part there is only dense blackness after the twilight is gone. Newspapers have been agitating to introduce "public lamps" in order to "secure [both] our persons from insult and abuse and our property from robbery and violence." It was seventeen years ago that Philadelphia established a municipal system of whale-oil lights mounted on wooden posts. Lamp-lighters were hired; fines were assessed against anyone who broke the lamps. Many local citizens wish Boston would do the same.

Some of the redcoats have noticed that most of the

dogs roaming the streets are small. Upon inquiry, they
learn there's a town ordinance restricting the height of
all dogs to ten inches. The ordinance was passed in
1728 after butchers complained that the larger animals
were making off with slaughtered carcasses that had
been hung up to cure. There are a few exceptions,
however. Sam Adams has an enormous Newfound-
land, "Queque," whose gentle manner has never
caused any problem. Its size is simply overlooked.

Fire is a constant threat to the people of Boston—
blazes are numerous. The most disastrous one occurred eight years ago, when more than four hundred
buildings were destroyed. It was a frightening experience for everyone. Hundreds lost not only their homes
but most of their belongings. After this conflagration,
town officials directed that all new structures must be
built of stone and roofed with slate or tile; otherwise
the owner would be fined fifty pounds. In addition a
curfew was established, and still remains in effect. At 9
P.M. the ringing of a bell warns townsfolk to extinguish
their hearth fires and put out all candlelight until 4:30
the following morning.

Boston has ten engine companies, each manned by a
captain and a company of twenty men. However,
citizens are expected to assist at fires too. Each
householder must keep one or more leather buckets

near his front door. When bells ring insistently or shouts are heard, everyone rushes to the scene. A double line is formed to the nearest well or cistern. The brimming buckets are passed up one row, the empties returned down the other.

Accumulations of soot in the chimneys probably cause most of the fires. A town committee was recently appointed to study the problem. It has recommended that anyone refusing to have his chimney swept out after forty-eight hours' notice, or anyone whose chimney starts a conflagration, be fined ten shillings.

The British soldiers are finding there is little by way of formal entertainment. All theater is banned, though occasionally a strolling group of players slips into town and gives a performance before it is evicted.

Social life for the men centers around the taverns. Night after night they gather in the smoke-blackened rooms to drink their rum punch and discuss politics. Luke Vardy, proprietor of the Royal Exchange Tavern across from the Town House, has welcomed the newly arrived officers from England. The tavern closely resembles those they have frequented at home; it has already become their favorite rendezvous. The Patriots prefer the Bunch of Grapes (with its three gilded clusters of grapes hanging over the door), on the south side of King Street—or the Green Dragon, not far

from Faneuil Hall. Along the waterfront, dock workers and sailors congregate at the Sun and Half-Moon.

Forty-two bookshops in town attest to the fact that
the sixteen thousand inhabitants are avid readers. And
of course there are the newspapers, four of them. The
Evening Post and the *News-Letter* give unbiased
reports. But last year John Mein began publishing a
twice-weekly paper, *The Chronicle,* which is read
primarily by the Tories; Mein always supports Crown
officials.

However, it is the weekly *Boston Gazette* that has the
widest circulation. Editors Benjamin Edes and John
Gill are fearless in their criticism of Royal policies. On
Sunday evenings the dingy little office at the corner of
Queen Street and Dassett Alley buzzes with activity.
Patriots gather here to help prepare the paper—writ-
ing articles (usually signing them with a pseudonym)
and offering suggestions.

John Adams, who is almost always present, writes in
his diary that this is "a curious employment, cooking
up paragraphs . . . working the political engine!"
Governor Bernard hates the *Gazette* and has reported
to Parliament that it "teems with Publications of the
most daring nature, denying the Authority of the
Supreme Legislature and tending to excite the people
to an Opposition of its Laws."

With Boston's sixteen churches, religion plays a powerful part in the community. There is strict observance of the Sabbath, which begins at 6 P.M. on Saturday. All work ceases; stores are closed; the Town Gate is locked. For the next twenty-four hours no one is permitted to do anything for pleasure or profit. Playing games or strolling on the Common is forbidden. Bells call the people to church services twice on Sunday, once in the morning and again in the afternoon.

However, since the arrival of the military, British officers have been showing little respect for the Lord's Day. Services are interrupted by the noise of soldiers drilling in the streets—the shouted commands, the rattle of muskets, the precise clump of army boots on the cobblestones. Already Lieutenant Colonel Dalrymple has received many complaints from the citizenry.

tension and tragedy

december 1768–february 1770

A mood of restlessness pervades Boston during the next few months. Although no riots flare up, the threat of one is always present. There are almost daily confrontations—a citizen roughly shouldered aside by a soldier, a redcoat cursed by a townsman, a young apprentice hurling a stick at one of the sentries. Even when there are no incidents, the continual presence of the hated Britishers reminds the citizenry that theirs is an occupied town, that Parliament intends to make the power of the Crown felt by the enforcement of its customs laws.

Daytime military activities rankle. John Adams, who

recently rented a house near Brattle Square, complains in his diary about the daily drilling of a regiment in the square. "The spirit-stirring drum and the ear-piercing Fife," he writes, arouse him and his family very early in the morning; he is angered by "the indigestion they excite."

Sentries with fixed bayonets are posted at the barracks, in front of officers' quarters, and at various other places around the town. It is their practice to challenge citizens who walk outside after dark. "Who goes there?" is the insolent question. More often than not, the pedestrian refuses to reply—or if he does, he adds some abusive language.

Packs of rowdy youngsters enjoy tormenting the troops. Jeering and whistling, the little boys taunt the redcoats by hurling snowballs and sharp chunks of ice. Often they yell, "Lobsters for sale! Who'll buy red lobsters today?" If a soldier grabs one of the young-sters and threatens to bash in his skull, the rowdies begin screaming, "Bloody backs! Bloody backs!" and scurry away to gather more snowballs.

A continuing irritant is the fact that Lieutenant Colonel Dalrymple has established his Main Guard post opposite the Town House. Two small cannon point directly at the chambers where the elected representatives convene. The people of Boston are particularly sensitive to threats, and the implication seems obvious. The Patriots maintain that the cannon are so placed as a warning to the assemblymen to be cautious in their deliberations. It's degrading, they say.

Comparative calm throughout the spring of 1769 encourages the military toward optimism. Tension eases somewhat. Early in June, General Thomas Gage, commander of all British troops in America, sends word to Lieutenant Colonel Dalrymple that some of the men are to return to England. Retain only the 14th and 29th Regiments, he orders. On July 4, the townspeople gather on the docks to cheer as the red-coats embark in waiting men-of-war.

With the departure of the soldiers many wonder why such large numbers of them were sent to Boston in the first place. There's popular clamor to get rid of all the redcoats immediately. The two remaining regiments become targets for more abuse. Crown officials find themselves faced with a dilemma. The soldiers were sent to Boston "to protect Royal author-ity"; now the officials must find a way to protect the men from the anger of the town.

Meanwhile, the Patriots are doing everything possi-ble to harass Governor Bernard. The *Boston Gazette* publishes article after article about his ineptness. He is accused of trying to establish himself "in the character of a Dictator." Finally the governor realizes that he can no longer be effective; he asks Parliament to relieve him. On August 1, he sails for home, leaving his wife and children to follow later. The townspeople celebrate Bernard's departure with flag waving, cannon blasts, and a huge bonfire on Fort Hill. Benjamin Edes, editor of the *Gazette,* observes in his next issue: "All the bells in town were rung for joy." Further, he declares that for nine years Francis Bernard "has been a Scourge to this Province, a Curse to North America, and a Plague to the whole Empire."

The official replacement for Bernard is Lieutenant Governor Thomas Hutchinson. A colonial aristocrat, born and reared in America, Hutchinson is a member of one of Boston's oldest and wealthiest families. After graduation from Harvard, he entered politics—Tory politics, as had his father and grandfather before him. He believes that only a few well-born and well-educated men like himself are destined to rule the colonies; all his offices have been held "by appointment." Though he is conscientious in his pursuit of duty, the Patriots look upon Hutchinson as a grasping and avaricious man, whose only desire is to please Crown authorities.

Now that Governor Bernard and part of the troops have left Boston, General Gage writes to Secretary

Hillsborough in London: "I should be glad to relieve the Troops from the oppression they are said to suffer where they are, and save a deal of vexatious trouble by removing them to places where they would be less obnoxious; amongst people better disposed and less turbulent." Hillsborough ignores the offer; the obnoxious soldiers remain as an ever-present threat to the peaceful community.

Throughout the fall, turmoil increases. Sam Adams finds that a number of the merchants who signed the Non-Importation Agreements have broken their promises. They are beginning to stock their shelves with goods from England. By January 1770, several of the Patriot leaders are encouraging the picketing of such stores. Posts with lettered hands pointing to the shop doors of the offenders are mysteriously erected; insulting placards are attached to these posts. Young boys pelt customers with dirt; windows are tarred and feathered. The sign is not removed until the guilty merchant forfeits his imported goods and publicly swears to observe the Agreements. The Tories suspect that the Patriots are encouraging the rowdies in their destructive tactics. Yet no one can prove it.

On Thursday, February 22, the inevitable explosion occurs. It's market day as well as a school holiday, and Dock Square is swarming with people of all ages. A

group of young roughnecks discovers that a post has been erected with a hand pointing to the shop of Theophilus Lillie. Looking for excitement, the boys surround the store and allow no one to enter. About 10 A.M., Ebenezer Richardson, a neighbor of Lillie's, appears in the street. He's a well-known informer for the British customs officers, and has been heard to say that he hopes the soldiers "will cut up the damned Yankees."

Angered at the sight of the post, Richardson stops the driver of a horse and wagon and tries to persuade him to ram against the sign. The driver refuses. A passing charcoal vendor also declines. In desperation, Richardson seizes the reins of a third vehicle and attempts to topple the post himself.

This commotion attracts the boys. They leave Lillie's shop and begin flinging stones, sticks, and dirt at the frenzied man. Richardson retreats toward his house, but spots some older faces in the crowd. Turning around, he shouts, "By the Eternal God, I'll make it too hot for you before tonight." The crowd only jeers as Richardson slams his front door.

The boys continue their barrage of fruit peelings, oyster shells, and street rubbish. Richardson reappears at the door, brandishing a stick. "Go off! Go off!" he shouts. "If you don't, I'll make a lane through you!"

As he steps back into the house, a brickbat is tossed through a window. The tinkle of breaking glass encourages the boys. Sticks, stones, and eggs begin flying from every direction. More people appear and join in the siege.

Inside the house a friend, George Wilmot, is waiting. He tells Richardson he will stand by him and asks for a gun. While the homeowner searches for weapons, the rock barrage increases. All the glass is broken; the leading and frames of the windows are smashed out.

Through a second-story window the crowd sees Richardson and Wilmot holding muskets. Richardson comes to the sill, kneels, and rests the barrel of his gun on the jagged ledge. Out on the street, eleven-year-old Christopher Snider stoops over to snatch another stone.

The crowd continues its taunts; no one believes that Richardson will fire. Taking careless aim, the over-wrought man pulls the trigger, reloads, and fires again several times. Sammy Gore is hit in the thigh, but is not seriously injured. Young Snider, however, is severely wounded by eleven bullets in the chest and abdomen.

Spectators pick up the bleeding boy and carry him into a nearby house. Someone is sent to inform

Snider's parents. Dr. Warren is summoned. After examining the lad, the doctor shakes his head. Nothing can be done, he says; the boy is dying.

At the first sound of gunfire, the bells of the New Brick Church have begun tolling. People now come running from all directions. The crowd batters down the front door and pours into the house to corner the culprits. Wilmot does not resist, but Richardson grabs a cutlass and brandishes it at his would-be captors. Eventually he is overpowered and muscled into the street, along with Wilmot. Someone brings a noose and suggests hanging.

Will Molineux is one of the spectators. Not wanting the Patriots to be blamed for a lynching, he steps forward. Any action taken, he says, must be legal. Let a justice of the peace pronounce punishment for these men.

Molineux's words have a calming effect. Instead of killing the men outright, the mob drags the two through the streets until they reach Faneuil Hall. Here four justices—Ruddock, Dana, Quincy, and Pemberton—hear the witnesses, and send Wilmot and Richardson to jail to await trial on March 13. A thousand spectators crowded into the chamber cheer lustily as the two men are led away under heavy guard.

On Monday, February 26, a great public funeral is

held for Christopher Snider. Sam Adams says it is "the largest perhaps ever known in America." A light snow is falling as the crowd begins collecting at 5 P.M. under the Liberty Tree, the towering elm on the corner of Newbury and Essex Streets that has become a gathering place for Patriot activities. A large board has been erected with the Biblical quotation, "Thou shalt take no satisfaction for the life of a MURDERER—he shall surely be put to death."

Nearly five hundred schoolboys line up, two by two, and begin the solemn march to the Old Granary Burying Ground. Six lads carry the coffin, followed by more than two thousand mourners. Thirty carriages, filled with wealthy merchants, bring up the rear. It's a somber and impressive sight, which John Adams describes in his diary thus: "This Shews there are many more Lives to spend if wanted in the Service of their Country. It Shews, too, that the Faction is not yet expiring—that the Ardor of the People is not to be quelled by the Slaughter of one Child and the Wounding of another."

Editor Benjamin Edes takes occasion to eulogize the lad in today's issue of the *Boston Gazette.* "Young as he was," writes Edes, "he died in his Country's Cause, by the Hand of an execrable Villain, directed by others, who could not bear to see the Enemies of America

made the *Ridicule of Boys.*" Further, Edes states that
the Patriots hope Snider's death "will be a means for
the future of preventing any, but more especially the
Soldiery, from being too free in the Use of their
Instruments of Death."

confrontation at
gray's ropewalk

march 2, 1770

One of the greatest problems for the British officers is
that of desertion, a practice which began in the earliest
days of the occupation. Lured by promises of farm land
and an opportunity to start a new life, the soldiers are
now slipping away in greater numbers than ever
before. General Gage, worried by this continuing
trend, writes Lieutenant Colonel Dalrymple to suggest
that he "throw out hints amongst them that the King
will Reward his Officers and Soldiers with the Estates
of the Rebels." Such hints have no effect; desertion
remains rampant.

Dalrymple would like to believe that once the

deserters have tried out their new-found freedom, they will prefer to return to the military. Such has not been the case so far. When the commanding officer sends out a detachment to recapture several privates who have stolen away from their units, the country people react quickly. Smearing soot on their faces so they cannot be identified, the farmers overpower the soldiers and rescue the deserters. Dalrymple is confounded. How can he combat this active resistance?

Resentment of the soldiers' presence continues to rise. Yet the officers find themselves in a dangerous position. British law forbids them to use their firearms without permission from Acting Governor Hutchinson or someone else in civil authority. The red-coated sentinels have been instructed never to do anything that will provoke open conflict with the citizenry. And, it must be admitted, the discipline has been strict.

Nevertheless, to walk through the streets—especially after dark—can be dangerous. The more militant Patriots are beginning to carry cudgels or canes to fend off any "insult," whether verbal or physical. No blood has yet been shed by the soldiers, but there are constant provocations. "Lobsters for sale! . . .Lo—obsters, who'll buy?" taunt the street urchins. Infuriated, the soldiers retort with their degrading nicknames for the civilians, yelling back, "Damned mohairs! . . . Boogers! . . . Yankees!"

Everyone expects an explosion—but when? Dr. Samuel Cooper, minister of the Brattle Street Church, receives a letter from Benjamin Franklin, who is in London. He's been "in constant panic," writes Franklin, ever since the troops arrived in Boston seventeen months ago.

Now, as February fades into March, there are only six hundred redcoats garrisoned in the town. Sam Adams, in a private meeting with other Patriot leaders, points out that the people of Boston, if properly armed, could easily drive the troops out. In addition, there's the alarm signal atop Beacon Hill. By lighting this tar barrel, the Patriots would be able to alert thousands of musket-bearing farmers who would flock to the town's support.

No matter how much Adams would like to see the soldiers leave, he is not yet ready for open warfare. Harassing individual redcoats is one thing, but firing on the Crown troops would be quite another matter. This would be judged treason in the eyes of King George III. Perhaps, the Patriot leader adds, something will happen that will make the town appear to be the injured party, not the military.

An incident that is more than a casual encounter develops on March 2. Just around the corner from the 29th Regiment's barracks is John Gray's ropewalk, consisting of five long open-air sheds. Here cordage is manufactured—the ropes and cables used to secure ships to the docks and lift heavy cargo onto the vessels. In each shed are massive conical spools. After dipping the hemp into enormous kettles bubbling with hot tar, the workers take the strands of tough fiber and wind them around the spools, pulling steadily to make tight, even ropes. It's rough work and demands men with strong muscles.

Employment at the ropewalk is spasmodic. Laborers are hired only when the owner has orders to be filled. Because the British privates are poorly paid—just a few shillings a month—they often seek odd jobs around town to supplement their meager salaries. Sometimes they work for nothing more than a drink or a square meal.

About 11 A.M. on this Friday, March 2, Private Walker of the 29th Regiment saunters by the ropewalk. One of the employees, William Green, looks up. "Soldier, do you want work?" he asks.

"Yes, I do, faith," answers Walker.

Green, leering at the redcoat, suggests that Walker clean his outhouse. Walker takes a mighty swing at the ropemaker—and misses. Nicholas Ferriter, employed only for today's work, rushes up from behind and grabs the private's coat; a cutlass drops out. The humiliated Walker, swearing vengeance, turns and runs toward the 29th's barracks while the laborers roar with laughter.

Within a few minutes Walker returns, accompanied by nine other privates. The redcoats advance belligerently, fists clenched. As the fight breaks out, the workers call for assistance. From the adjoining shed more ropemakers pour in. They've armed themselves with wouldring sticks, those sturdy hardwood tools used to twist the conical spools on which the rope is wound. The soldiers are soon driven off, and retreat to their barracks.

The ropemakers are in a jocular mood, laughing among themselves about how easily the soldiers have given up. But before the merriment subsides, some forty redcoats are sighted running toward the rope-walk, armed with clubs and sticks, shouting and cursing as they advance. The workers grab their weapons and the battle begins once again. Private Matthew Killroy, a particularly troublesome soldier, sees one of the ropemakers alone. Killroy knocks the man down and begins beating him with his cudgel, while the other regulars surge into the open shed and aim blows at the workers.

The noise of flailing sticks mingled with screams attracts the attention of Justice of the Peace John Hill, who lives nearby. He comes running and commands

that peace be restored at once. Neither the soldiers nor the ropeworkers pay any attention.

The fighting continues for several more minutes, until the redcoats are driven out of the shed and up Green's Lane toward their barracks. A corporal attached to the 29th Regiment realizes the seriousness of the encounter and orders the privates to report to their quarters on the double. Nursing black eyes and bloody noses as well as counting missing teeth, the soldiers immediately go to work sharpening cutlasses and shaping cudgels. They intend to be well prepared when another opportunity arises for revenge.

By Saturday morning, all Boston is buzzing about the affair at John Gray's ropewalk. People cluster in small groups on the streets to talk about what has happened. Over at Daniel Calfe's store, conversation turns to yesterday's incident. The soldiers are to blame, the customers agree. One shopper, however, cannot smother her anger. Mrs. James McDeed, the wife of a grenadier in the 29th Regiment, shakes her fist at Calfe. "The soldiers were in the right," she declares, "and before Tuesday or Wednesday night next they will wet their swords or bayonets in New England people's blood!"

Meanwhile, Lieutenant Colonel Maurice Carr, commander of the 29th, alarmed by the violent confrontation, writes to Acting Governor Hutchinson. Carr protests the ropewalk incident and complains that his men are required to endure continual abuse from the citizens. Hutchinson calls a Council meeting and presents the letter from Carr. What assistance will the members offer? he asks. "None whatsoever," is the unanimous reply. The people will never be satisfied until the troops are removed, Hutchinson is told.

Despite the friction between soldiers and civilians, there are some few Britishers who have become friendly with the townspeople. On Sunday evening, Private Charles Malone goes to the home of Mr. Amos Thayer and asks to speak with him. Malone is told by Thayer's sister, Mary, that Amos is otherwise engaged.

"I have great regard for your brother," says the soldier. "I came on purpose to tell him to keep in his house, for before Tuesday night next at twelve o'clock, there will be a great deal of bloodshed, and a great many lives lost. By keeping in his house he will be well out of harm's way." Before the astonished Mistress Thayer can reply, Malone turns and disappears into the darkness.

Now the rumors become more and more threatening. Rev. Andrew Eliot of the New North Church warns several of his parishioners that he has known since Saturday that "many townspeople are looking forward to fighting it out with the soldiers on Monday." He adds that bells will be rung as an alarm.

There's little doubt now that a showdown is inevitable.

the massacre

march 5, 1770

Boston is blanketed with snow on this frigid Monday morning, March 5. Nearly a foot has fallen during the past few days. In the middle of King Street, busiest thoroughfare in town, traffic has packed down the snow and it is mixed with gravel and seashells. During the night the packed snow has turned to ice, making footing treacherous for those who are out early.

Workers, slipping and sliding down toward the docks, are amazed to find posters tacked all along the waterfront. They read:

Boston, March 5, 1770
This is to Inform the Rebellious People in Boston that

the Soldyers in the 14th and 29th Regiments are determined to Joine together and defend themselves against all who shall Oppose them.

Signed: the SOLDYERS OF THE 14TH and 29TH REGIMENTS

Who wrote the posters and when they were put up remains a mystery. The more conservative citizens suspect it was not the soldiers themselves. Rather they wonder if someone is trying to provoke trouble—someone who wants to get rid of the troops.

At 11 A.M., the changing of the guard takes place, a daily ceremony executed with strict military discipline. The 29th Regiment is on duty today, with Captain Thomas Preston in charge. Preston is a forty-year-old Irishman; even the Patriots admit that he's a sober, honest man and a good officer. Private Hugh White takes his post near a small sentry box at the corner of King Street and Royal Exchange Lane, where he will keep watch over the Custom House. Lieutenant James Basset commands the Main Guardhouse, the British military headquarters to the south of the Town House across a narrow fork of King Street. A squad marches out to Boston Neck to relieve the men on duty there; other sentries take up positions at various places considered by Crown officials to be important to the welfare of the town.

By midafternoon the sun has broken through the clouds and melted some of the snow; little rivulets begin trickling through the streets and alleys. But later the temperature drops. An icy crust spreads over the snow; icicles form on overhanging eaves. As darkness falls, a thin quarter moon appears in the now cloudless sky. Its light, reflected on the snow, gives an eerie brilliance to the shadowy streets.

After supper there seem to be more people roaming the town than is usual for such a cold night. Swaggering soldiers jostle the townsmen, threatening them with cudgels and bayonets. In turn, the citizens respond with jeers and taunts. One of the regulars is heard to say that there are "them in Boston as would eat their supper Monday night would never eat another." Sam Adams has spent the day making his usual round of the taverns to talk politics. He's thrown out veiled hints that there may be trouble tonight, that farmers in the surrounding area have already been alerted.

Around 8 P.M., Private White is pacing up and down in front of the Custom House. Captain Lieutenant John Goldfinch of the 14th Regiment passes and the sentry salutes. Just at that moment, a young wigmaker's apprentice, Edward Garrick, sees Goldfinch and shouts, "There goes the fellow that won't pay my master for dressing his hair." Goldfinch, knowing he has the receipt in his pocket, refuses to acknowledge the insult.

Private White, however, retorts that all British officers are gentlemen; they pay whatever they owe. The saucy apprentice continues to taunt the sentry: there are no gentlemen in that regiment, he scoffs.

White leaves his post and walks over to the boy. "Let me see your face," he commands.

"I'm not ashamed to show my face," is Garrick's impudent reply.

Swinging his musket angrily, White strikes the side of Garrick's head. The blow knocks the boy onto the icy street. Screaming with pain, he gets up and staggers off, clutching his bleeding wound.

About this same time, citizens Francis Archibald and William Merchant, walking along Brattle Street, pass Murray's Barracks, in which the 29th Regiment is quartered. They meet a soldier who is brandishing a broadsword "of uncommon size," as it is later described. Archibald turns on the redcoat. "Put up your cutlass," he says. "It is not right to carry it at this time of night."

"Damn you, you Yankee boogers, what's your business?" the soldier challenges them, striking Archibald on the arm, and thrusting his sword into Merchant's coat.

Suddenly ten or twelve soldiers come rushing out of

the barracks, armed with tongs, shovels, and bayonets. The noise attracts passersby, and they join the struggle. Soon the street is filled with regulars and townsmen, wielding whatever weapons they can find. Fearing a riot, several British officers attempt to push the soldiers back into their barracks. At this moment Boston merchant Richard Palmes approaches one of the officers and tells him that the redcoats are not allowed out after 8 P.M.

"Pray, do you mean to teach us our duty?" the officer inquires.

"I do not," Palmes answers hastily; "only to remind you of it."

Within a few minutes the officers succeed in getting their men back to quarters. Now they assure the citizens that the soldiers will not be allowed outside again tonight.

"You mean they dare not come out!" someone shouts. "You dare not let them out."

Palmes, acting as a peacemaker, turns to his fellow townsmen: "Gentlemen, you hear what the officers say, and you had better go home."

A few take Palmes' advice, but most in the crowd are looking for more excitement. "Away to the Main Guard!" is the outcry. The men surge down the alley toward King Street, huzzahing and rapping the side walls with their cudgels. Young boys race up and down yelling, "Town-born, turn out! Town-born, turn out!"

Meanwhile, a throng of about two hundred has gathered in Dock Square. Armed with wooden staves and sticks of all kinds, the men mill aimlessly about the square, hooting and cheering. Those who have no weapons break into the market stalls and rip off legs of the produce tables and butchers' blocks.

When a mysterious stranger in a white wig and red cloak appears in their midst, the crowd quiets down to listen. He is obviously inciting the mob to action. Once the speech is finished the stranger slips away, as the men shout, "To the Main Guard!" Shrieking that they'll "do for the soldiers," the mob roars up Royal Exchange Lane toward the Town House.

At this moment, the bells in the Brattle Street Church begin ringing wildly. Other churches echo the alarm for fire. Men all over town grab up their leather buckets and head for King Street. Shouts of "Fire! Fire!" pierce the cold night air.

Seventeen-year-old Samuel Maverick, an apprentice to an ivory turner, is having supper with Jonathan Cary and his four sons. At the first sound of the bells, the boys jump up from the table and rush into the street.

Over at Thomas Symmonds' victualing house,

Crispus Attucks has just finished his evening meal. The huge mulatto—he stands six feet two inches—arrived less than an hour ago on a whaling ship and is here awaiting passage to North Carolina. He is always ready to participate in a good fight. Hearing the insistent peal of bells, Attucks summons sailors from the other tables and suggests they join in discovering what's going on. Led by the burly mulatto, the sailors head down toward the Town House, each man carrying a heavy cordwood stick, holding it over his head like a banner.

Now, at 9 P.M., men and boys are streaming into King Street from every direction. A crowd has already gathered around the Custom House; for the last few minutes they've been pelting the sentry, Private White, with snowballs, sticks, and chunks of ice. Suddenly young Garrick, the wigmaker's apprentice, bobs up and points an accusing finger at the sentry.

"There he is! There's the one that knocked me down!"

The mob presses forward. "Tar and feather him!" someone shouts.

"Kill him, kill him, the bloody brute!"

Badly frightened, Private White runs up the Custom House steps while the crowd continues to shower him with icy missiles. In desperation White loads his musket and levels it at the people standing below him.

Frenzied spectators begin screaming: "He's going to shoot!" . . . "Fire and be damned, ye bloody rascal!"

Instead of pulling the trigger, the redcoat shrieks at the top of his voice, "Turn out the Main Guard! Turn out the Main Guard!"

Captain Thomas Preston, officer of the day at the guardhouse, hears the frantic cries of the sentry and orders Corporal William Wemms to take six privates and go to Hugh White's assistance. Forming up in a column of twos, William McCauley, Matthew Killroy, Hugh Montgomery, James Hartegan, William Warren, and John Carroll follow Corporal Wemms out of the guardhouse. The men march down King Street, muskets shouldered, bayonets fixed. Captain Preston, fearful that there may be violence, decides to go with his men.

Pushing and shoving their way through the spectators, the relief party heads for the Custom House steps. Here the soldiers fall in line, as sentry White joins them.

Captain Preston takes a stance in front of his men, shouting at the mob to disperse. He is barraged with curses and snowballs. The catcalls continue: "Why do you not fire?" . . . "Damn you, you dare not fire!" . . . "Fire and be damned!"

Richard Palmes, the citizen who tried to make peace

at Murray's Barracks a short time ago, now works his way through the mob to speak to Captain Preston. "Are your soldiers' guns loaded?" he asks.

"With powder and ball," Preston answers.

"Sir," says Palmes, "I hope you don't intend the soldiers shall fire on the inhabitants."

"By no means," the captain assures him. "By no means." Then he adds that he is standing directly before the musket muzzles. If the soldiers pull their triggers, he will "fall a sacrifice."

"My giving the word 'fire' under these circumstances would prove me no officer," Preston asserts.

Bookseller Henry Knox, watching the spectacle, edges up to Captain Preston. Clutching at the officer's coat sleeve, Knox pleads, "In God's name take your men back! The people are angry and there will be bloodshed. If you fire upon them, your life must answer for the consequence."

"I am sensible of that," Preston retorts, and turns away.

Now the crowd has grown to alarming proportions. It presses in upon the soldiers, voices challenging them to put down their weapons and fight, jeering that the redcoats are "cowardly rascals." Confused by the uproar and distracted by the taunts, the soldiers tremble with rage.

Crispus Attucks and his fellow sailors are standing in the forefront of the mob. Suddenly, Attucks hurls his heavy cordwood stick at Private Montgomery, knocking the soldier onto the ice and sending his musket flying. A violent scuffle for the weapon follows; Montgomery retrieves his gun and takes aim. Shouts ring out: "Fire!" "Fire!" "Fire, if you dare!"

The sharp crack of gunfire pierces the air. Attucks pitches forward into the snow, a bullet in his chest. For two seconds there is total silence. Then Private Killroy raises his weapon and fires aimlessly into the crowd. One by one, in ragged succession, the other five follow Killroy's lead.

Sam Gray, a ropewalk laborer, falls dead. A bystander, sailor James Caldwell, is dropped by the gunfire. The young apprentice, Samuel Maverick, turns and dashes toward the Town House, but a wild bullet bounces off the icy cobblestones and strikes him in the head. He crumples over, dying. Patrick Carr is heading for a barber shop at the corner of Quaker Lane when a shot tears through his hip; he tumbles down, gravely wounded. A friend carries him into a house in Fitch's Alley. Six others are sprawled on the snow, injured by the soldiers' reckless shots.

For a brief moment the crowd is silent. Then the wildest confusion breaks out, as men and boys scram-

ble up side streets and alleys. A few remain behind to carry the dead and wounded to safety.

Infuriated, Captain Preston turns on his men. Why did they fire? he wants to know. The soldiers say they kept hearing the word "Fire!"—and assumed he was ordering them to shoot. Preston only shakes his head in despair, visibly upset by tonight's tragedy. The men are ordered to form up and withdraw to the Main Guardhouse.

aftermath of violence

march 5-6, 1770

Within minutes after the troops depart, bells in church steeples all over town begin clanging again. At the Main Guardhouse, regimental drums beat the call to arms. Cries of "Town-born, turn out!" sound through the night as hundreds of men begin pouring into King Street, carrying knives, cudgels, and wooden staves. Rumors fly everywhere—that the soldiers have fired into a peaceful crowd, that they've killed a hundred citizens or more.

Reports reach Captain Preston that several thousand townspeople are in the next street making preparations for an assault. Some warn that armed reinforcements have been alerted in the surrounding countryside. The captain orders the entire 29th Regiment to form up in King Street; one squad is placed before the Town House in kneeling position for street firing.

Over at Province House, Acting Governor Hutchinson is alarmed by the furious pealing of the bells. As he hustles into his greatcoat, there's an insistent pounding at the front door. Several breathless citizens urge Hutchinson to come quickly, or, they say, "the town will be all in blood."

Striding rapidly toward King Street, the acting governor finds himself in the midst of a mob of men who are pushing, shoving, cursing as they brandish their weapons in a threatening manner. Hutchinson elbows his way up to Captain Preston and confronts the officer with a barrage of questions. What provoked the tragedy? Did the captain order the soldiers to fire? In a scathing voice he continues, "Do you know, sir, you have no power to fire on any body of the people collected together except you have a civil magistrate with you to give orders?" Turning away angrily, Preston refuses to answer.

Several in the crowd recognize Hutchinson. Shouts ring out demanding to know what action he will take. The people must be satisfied with his answer or they will take matters into their own hands. The push of the mob increases as the acting governor finds himself propelled toward the Town House door. Hesitantly he mounts the stairway to the second floor and goes out to the balcony overlooking the crowd below.

The people quiet down—watching, waiting. Now Thomas Hutchinson expresses his concern that more violence can only lead to a worse catastrophe. If the soldiers are found guilty, they will be punished as the law requires. Further, he emphasizes, "the law shall have its course; I will live and die by the law." Then he promises there will be a thorough inquiry tomorrow.

But the crowd wants action tonight. Arrest Preston, voices cry, and send the soldiers back to their quarters. Hutchinson raises both hands in a gesture of despair. He cannot give orders to the military, he explains. At this moment, Lieutenant Colonel Dalrymple, commander of all Boston troops, appears on the balcony and confers hurriedly with the acting governor.

Stepping forward, Dalrymple leans over and shouts orders to the soldiers below. The redcoats arise from their kneeling position in front of the Town House, shoulder arms, and form up to march back to their barracks. Hutchinson then announces that he will issue a warrant for the sheriff to bring Captain Preston and the eight soldiers here for an immediate inquiry—this very hour.

Slowly the milling crowd begins drifting away, though some push through the Town House door and into the Council chamber to make certain that Hutchinson keeps his promise. Justices Richard Dana and John Tudor are summoned, but it is almost midnight when the interrogation begins. For the next few hours the justices examine the evidence, listening to the testimony of witnesses, questioning Preston and the eight soldiers. By 3 A.M., it is apparent there is sufficient reason to imprison the redcoats. Under heavy guard the Britishers are escorted to the new stone jail on Queen Street.

Earlier in the evening, when the bells of Old South Meeting House began ringing, John Adams was attending a meeting of his political club at the home of Henderson Inches. The men grabbed their coats and rushed into the street to assist in putting out the flames. Instead they learned that British soldiers had fired into a crowd of civilians, that some were killed, others wounded.

Adams' first concern was for his wife, Abigail. She was at home alone with the children, and noise always frightened his little family. He edged around the crowd at the Town House and slipped up Boylston's Alley into Brattle Square. There in the street was a company of soldiers, muskets shouldered and bayonets fixed. Only a narrow space had been left for pedestrians.

John, fearing that he might be challenged, walked hurriedly past. But the redcoats stood like statues, eyes straight ahead.

Now at home, Adams finds that Abigail has recovered from her initial fright at the commotion outside. The two sit quietly, discussing the implications of this latest crisis. For months, John points out, his cousin Sam Adams and Dr. Warren have been inflaming the prejudices of "the lower orders"—those laborers and dock workers who are always ready to riot. Tonight men have been killed. It's almost certain that the people of Boston will demand the blood of the soldiers in retaliation. However, the lawyer emphasizes, if the soldiers were under orders or acted in self-defense, they must be protected by the law.

There's another complication too. How will the other New England colonies view tonight's tragedy? There are many Patriots in these colonies who consider Boston a disorderly community. Has the Patriot cause been shattered by an insolent mob goading the soldiers to action? There is only one way, John tells Abigail, that the bad impression of the town can be erased. The soldiers must receive a fair trial. If innocent, they must be acquitted. Then it will be apparent that Boston has taken an impartial stand, placing the law above all prejudice.

It is nearly dawn before Adams succumbs to a few hours of restless sleep. Arising early on this morning after the massacre, he hurries over to his law office near the Town House. He is engrossed in preparing a brief when there is a frantic pounding on the door. John calls out, "Enter!" and a man stumbles in, his eyes streaming with tears. The lawyer recognizes James Forrest, a prosperous merchant who has been active in Tory politics.

Forrest is almost hysterical. "I come," he gasps, "with a very solemn message from a very unfortunate man, Captain Preston in prison. He wishes for counsel and can get none."

Struggling to regain his composure, Forrest explains that he has already called on three Crown lawyers— naturally he approached them first. But they have all refused to take the case, fearing the vengeance of the Patriots. Robert Auchmuty, a judge of the Vice-Admiralty Court and supporter of the Crown, has said he will act for Preston, but only if John Adams will serve as counsel with him. Josiah Quincy, Jr., has given the same answer.

Without hesitation Adams says, "Counsel ought to be the very last thing that an accused person should [lack] in a free country. The bar ought in my opinion to be independent and impartial at all times and in every circumstance. Persons whose lives are at stake ought to have the counsel they prefer."

Silent for a few moments, the lawyer then adds that Captain Preston must understand that "this will be as important a cause as ever was tried in any court or country of the world, and that every lawyer must hold himself responsible not only to his country, but to the highest and most infallible of all tribunals for the part he should act."

The merchant nods in agreement. Further, Adams asserts, there will be no tricks, no lies, no pompous oratory in the courtroom. The client can expect "nothing more than fact, evidence, and law will justify."

"Captain Preston requests and desires no more," says Forrest. "As God Almighty is my Judge, I believe him an innocent man."

"That must be ascertained by his trial," Adams replies. "And if he thinks he cannot have a fair trial of that issue without my assistance, he shall have it."

Forrest springs up and grasps the lawyer's hand in gratitude. Groping in first one pocket, then another, he finally pulls out a single guinea and offers it as a retaining fee. John Adams accepts it solemnly. The lawyer realizes he is taking a bold step. He will undoubtedly receive criticism from his Patriot friends;

yet he wants to prove to the world that law and justice can be upheld in Boston. This is his great opportunity!

Since early this morning, farmers have been swarming into town across Boston Neck. Most of them carry muskets with small bundles of clothing tied to the barrels. It's obvious that messages were dispatched last night to the surrounding countryside; the people have responded to the warnings.

Notices are posted for a town meeting to convene at 11 A.M. By that hour Faneuil Hall is jammed with both local citizens and farmers, all of whom demand that the military occupation of Boston end at once. A committee of fifteen is appointed to call upon Acting

Governor Hutchinson. Sam Adams, as chairman, drafts the resolution to be presented. It reads:

> That it is the unanimous opinion of this meeting that the inhabitants and soldiery can no longer live together in safety; that nothing can rationally be expected to restore the peace of the town and prevent further blood and carnage but the immediate removal of the troops; and that we therefore must fervently pray his honor that his power and influences may be asserted for their instant removal.

The committee leaves at once for the Town House to confer with Hutchinson and his Council. More and more people jam into Faneuil Hall, waiting for the acting governor's reply. Hours pass with no word. By 3 P.M., there are nearly four thousand men spilling out into Dock Square. Dr. Warren suggests that they move to the Old South Meeting House, where everyone can be accommodated.

It is nearly 4 P.M. when Sam Adams and his committee return to the town meeting with their report. An expectant hush settles over the audience as Adams mounts the platform. In a voice shaking with anger, he says that Hutchinson has refused their demands, excusing himself on grounds that he can give no orders to the King's troops. Because Castle William is acknowledged as a part of the town, one regiment—

the 29th—could be quartered there, but the 14th Regiment must continue to occupy Boston, at least until further orders are received from General Gage in New York.

Peering intently at the four thousand seated in the meeting house, Sam Adams now puts the question: shall this offer be accepted?

The crowd roars its disapproval.

"No!" "No!"

"Both regiments or none!"

"Not one, but two!"

A new committee is appointed to return to Hutchinson with the people's answer. Adams leads the delegation out of the meeting house, followed by Will Molineux, William Phillips, Dr. Joseph Warren, Joshua Henshaw, John Hancock, and Samuel Pemberton.

A light snow has begun falling on the icy streets, creating hazardous walking as the men head back to the Town House. When they enter the second-floor Council chamber, they find all twenty-eight members seated around the oval table. For this occasion the councilmen have donned full dress—massive white wigs, English scarlet cloth coats, and gold-laced hats. Lieutenant Colonel Dalrymple is also present.

Adams advances toward Hutchinson. "Sir," he says,

"if the lieutenant governor or Colonel Dalrymple, or both together, have authority to remove one regiment, they have the authority to remove two, and nothing short of a total evacuation of the town, by all the regular troops, will satisfy the public mind or preserve the peace of the province. The people demand it!"

Hutchinson's face pales. Sam Adams then adds that there are four thousand men waiting at the Old South Meeting House—and fifteen thousand more in the province are ready to rise up against the Crown, if the soldiers do not leave.

The acting governor scans the faces of his Council. Each man nods agreement: the troops must be removed if the peace of Boston is to be maintained. Hutchinson then beckons to Dalrymple, and the two hold a whispered conference.

After some minutes, the British commander turns to the committee. "I give you my word of honor," he asserts, "that I will begin my preparations in the morning. There will be no unnecessary delay in removing the whole of the two regiments to the castle." Sam Adams bows to the Council and signals his committee to follow him out of the chamber.

Back at Old South, the people wait patiently. No one wants to leave without knowing the outcome. The hall has grown quite dark, and the sexton now pushes

down the side aisles to light the candles in brass sconces along the walls. When the committee enters the meeting house door, there's a distinct rustle. The audience peers around, trying to fathom what Hutchinson's answer is. Sam Adams strides to the platform in silence, mounts the steps, and turns to the sea of faces. Smiling broadly, he pronounces, "Both regiments will go!"

Pandemonium breaks out. Cheers, huzzahs, shouts, echo through the meeting house. Men clap each other on the shoulders in joyous acclaim. At last, at long last, the town will be rid of the redcoats!

Before the meeting adjourns, a night watch is organized with civilian volunteers as guards. It will be several days before the soldiers can be moved out of their barracks. No one in all Boston wants any further rioting.

who is guilty?

march 7–22, 1770

It's cold on this Wednesday evening, March 7—a damp, chilling cold intensified by the strong east wind blowing in across the harbor. Nevertheless, the civilian night watch begins at 9 P.M.

John Adams was one of the first to volunteer at yesterday's town meeting, and he has been assigned the beat from the Custom House to Cornhill. Now, well bundled against the vicious weather, he sets out from the little house on Brattle Street. Across the upper part of his greatcoat is strapped a small tin lantern; over his right shoulder he carries a gun, the butt end grasped in his mittened hand. For the next eight hours he paces back and forth, peering into the darkness to make certain that no rioters lurk in the shadows. All over town other volunteers follow the same pattern, insuring peace for a sleeping Boston. As dawn breaks, the men blow out their lanterns and head home, relieved that there's been no trouble.

Precisely at 12 noon, all the church bells begin tolling—the slow, solemn tones for a funeral. The shops are closed; activity along the waterfront has ceased. A tremendous crowd has already gathered in King Street. Some say there are as many as four thousand people. Not only are local citizens here, but hundreds from the surrounding countryside have come to witness the funeral for the men killed by the British soldiers—"martyrs of a horrid massacre," Bostonians are calling them.

For the victims—Crispus Attucks, James Caldwell, Samuel Gray, and Samuel Maverick—separate hearses have been ordered. Now they converge before the Custom House, site of the tragedy three days ago. The mourners, six abreast, fall in behind the vehicles as the procession begins moving slowly up King Street toward the Old Granary Burying Ground. The leaders have chosen to file past the jail on Queen Street, where Captain Preston and the eight redcoats are held.

John Adams, marching alongside the other Patriots,

is saddened by the futile deaths of the four men. Yet he cannot help but wonder about the wisdom of such a dramatic procession. Will the fury of the townspeople permit his clients a fair trial? Has his cousin Sam gone too far in trying to arouse indignation? Fact and evidence must prevail in any court of law. But certainly John's job of saving the redcoats' lives has been made more difficult by today's ceremonies.

At the burying ground the procession halts. After appropriate remarks, the four coffins are lowered into a common grave. Josiah Quincy, Jr., standing nearby, catches the eye of lawyer Adams. Neither man changes expression, though each knows instinctively what the other is thinking.

On Saturday, March 10, the hour that the town has long awaited arrives. The streets are lined with jubilant spectators as His Majesty's 14th and 29th Regiments begin their march to Long Wharf. There ships are waiting to take the redcoats out to Castle William.

Hordes of small boys taunt the troops with cries of "Hup, hup, who buys lobsters?" Marching beside Lieutenant Colonel Dalrymple is the Patriot Will Molineux, who explains his presence by saying he wants "to protect the soldiers from the indignation of the people." Decked out in a tattered red and blue uniform with a three-cornered hat angled over one eye, Molineux provides comic relief as he bows good-

naturedly to the crowd. The spectators clap with delight. By contrast, the scowling redcoats look to neither right nor left, their faces sullen with resentment.

However, the removal of the regiments does not dispel the fever of anger. In fact, even the ministers are inciting the Patriots to further action. From the pulpit of the Old North Church, the young Rev. John Lathrop speaks of "sorrow for the dead, who fell victims to the merciless rage of wicked men; indignation against the worst of murderers." Further, he adds that if a man "really intended to kill, unless in defense of his own life under absolute necessity, *he shall surely be put to death.*"

On March 12 the weekly issue of the *Boston Gazette* appears, carrying a full account of the events of March 5. Heavy black rules border the front page. Paul Revere has made an engraving of the four coffins inscribed with death's heads and the victims' initials. The editors predict that evidence will be found "to open up such a scene of Villainy acted by a dirty Banditti, as must astonish the Public." In conclusion, they challenge their fellow townsmen:

> The Streets of Boston have already been bathed with the BLOOD of innocent Americans! Shed by the execrable Hands of the diabolical Tools of Tyrants!— O AMERICANS! this BLOOD calls aloud for VENGEANCE!

Readers of this issue of the newspaper are astonished by the "card," or advertisement, that has been printed on the front page:

> Boston-Gaol,
> Monday 12th March, 1770
>
> Messieurs Edes & Gill,
> Permit me thro' the Channel of your paper, to return my Thanks in the most publick Manner to the Inhabitants in general of this Town, who throwing aside *all Party* and Prejudice, have with the utmost Humanity and Freedom stept forth Advocates for Truth in Defence of my injured Innocence, in the late unhappy Affair that happened on Monday Night last: And to assure them, that I shall ever have the highest Sense of the *Justice* they have done me, which will ever be gratefully remembered, by
>
> Their most obliged and most
> obedient humble Servant,
> Thomas Preston.

People question what has prompted such a statement from the British captain. Is this some sort of trickery? Or is he merely trying to enlist sympathy?

A town meeting is called for the night of the 12th. James Bowdoin, Dr. Joseph Warren, and Samuel Pemberton are appointed to obtain "a particular Account of all proceedings relative to the Massacre in King Street on Monday Night last, that a full and Just representation may be made thereof."

The following day, the committee of three begins gathering its evidence. One by one, witnesses are brought before justices of the peace. After being sworn to tell the truth, they are questioned. There is no cross-examination. A clerk takes down the answers and the witness is then asked to sign the written version of his testimony, or "deposition."

Ninety-four of the ninety-six witnesses state their belief that the massacre resulted from a plot by the soldiers and customs commissioners. The ninety-fifth witness is Hammond Green. His testimony is neutral. The ninety-sixth witness, Thomas Greenwood, blames the citizens for the trouble. In the committee's report, however, a footnote is added, advising that "no credit be given to his deposition."

Meanwhile, a fifth victim of the Monday night tragedy, Patrick Carr, is dying from his bullet wounds. Now, on March 14, the man is urged by Dr. John Jeffries to make a deathbed statement.

"Were the soldiers abused?" the doctor asks.

"Yes," replies Carr. "I am surprised that they did not fire long before." Then he adds that he is a native of Ireland and has frequently seen riotous mobs, with soldiers called to quell them. He has often seen soldiers fire on people in Ireland, but never has he seen soldiers endure half so much before they fired.

With a final breath Carr forgives the soldier who

shot him, whoever he was. He is satisfied that the redcoat fired only in self-defense.

When news of the massacre reaches General Thomas Gage in New York City, he writes to Lieutenant Colonel Dalrymple immediately.

> It is absolutely Necessary every thing relating to the unhappy affair of the 5th of March, should appear as full as it is possible upon Captain Preston's Tryal. Not only what happened on the said Night, should be circumstantially made to appear, but also every Insult and Attack made upon the Troops, previous thereto, with the Pains taken by the Military to prevent Quarrells between the Soldiers and inhabitants. . . .

In response to General Gage's request, Dalrymple appoints officers to gather the necessary evidence. Within a week the report is complete; and on March 16, John Robinson, a customs commissioner, sails secretly for London. With him he carries military depositions that blame the town for the rowdy actions and subsequent shootings.

At a town meeting on March 19, the committee appointed the previous week presents its report, entitled: *A Short Narrative of the Horrid Massacre in Boston, Perpetrated in the Evening of the Fifth of March, 1770 by the Soldiers of the 29th Regiment Which with the 14th Regiment Were Then Quartered There: With*

Some Observations on the State of Things Prior to That Catastrophe.

To the men assembled in Faneuil Hall, James Bowdoin reads the account that he has written. In it he recalls the friendly relations that had existed between the Mother Country and her colonies until the Stamp Act and the Townshend duties were imposed. "The residence of the Commissioners here," he asserts, "has been detrimental, not only to the commerce, but to the political interests of the town and province; and not only so, but we can trace from it the causes of the late horrid massacre." Bowdoin then continues with a recounting of the events of the tragic night. In conclusion, he implies that a massacre of the townspeople was in the making, that the many threats from the redcoats were a part of a conspiracy. Attached to the narrative are the complete depositions of the ninety-six witnesses.

When the author has finished, the citizens at the town meeting cast a unanimous vote to accept the report. Edes and Gill are authorized to print the narrative. Copies are ordered sent to friends of America in London. Named specifically in the town clerk's minutes are: "the Right Honorable Isaac Barre, Esq., one of his Majesty's most Honorable Privy Council; Thomas Pownall, Esq., late the Governor of

Massachusetts; William Bolan, Esq., Agent for his Majesty's Council; Denny DeBerdt, Esq., Agent for the House of Representatives; Benjamin Franklin, Esq., LLD, and Barlow Trecothick, Esq., a member of Parliament for the city of London."

During these past few days, John Adams has had some exasperating moments. Patriots, indignant that he has accepted the defense of Captain Preston and the British soldiers, approach him and ask if what they've heard can possibly be true. Is he actually going to be counsel for murderers? John's temper flares. These men are to be assumed innocent, he says, until proven guilty.

Even more embarrassing is the attitude of the Crown officials. Many of them are convinced that lawyer Adams is sympathetic to their cause now and openly congratulate him.

Josiah Quincy, Jr., is finding opposition too. On March 22, he receives a letter from his father in Braintree. It reads:

> My Dear Son,
> I am under great affliction at hearing the bitterest reproaches uttered against you, for having become an advocate for those criminals who are charged with the murder of their fellow-citizens. Good Heavens! Is it possible? I will not believe it. . . . I have been told

that you have actually engaged for Captain Preston; and I have heard the severest reflections made upon the occasion, by men who had just before manifested the highest esteem for you, as one destined to be a saviour of your country.

I must own to you, it has filled the bosom of your aged and infirm parent with anxiety and distress, lest it should not only prove true, but destructive of your reputation and interest; and I repeat, I will not believe it, unless it be confirmed by your own mouth, or under your own hand.

Your anxious and distressed parent,
Josiah Quincy.

Though Josiah Jr. is saddened by his father's words, he is still resolved to continue as one of the defense counsel. In answer, he writes:

I have little leisure, and less inclination, either to know or [to] take notice of those ignorant slanderers who have dared to utter their "bitter reproaches" in your hearing against me, for having become an advocate for criminals charged with murder. . . .

Let such be told, Sir, that these criminals, charged with murder, are *not yet legally proved guilty,* and therefore, however criminal, are entitled, by the laws of God and man, to all legal counsel and aid. . . .

After the events of the past two weeks, Acting Governor Thomas Hutchinson is utterly dispirited. He feels he has lost complete control, and writes to General Gage in New York that "Government is at an end and in the hands of the people." Hutchinson adds that he stands "absolutely alone, no single person of my Council or any other person in authority affording me the least support."

In a letter to General Gage, Lieutenant Colonel Dalrymple confirms Hutchinson's gloomy outlook. Writing about the acting governor, Dalrymple reports:

> He has no earthly weight or power here; a proposal coming from him would be for that reason sure to miscarry. . . . If the people are disposed to any measure nothing more is necessary than for the multitude to assemble, for nobody dares oppose them or call them to account.

a town in turmoil

april – october 1770

Demands for revenge against "the murderers" race through Boston. Hostility is rampant. The Patriots, led by Sam Adams, agitate to bring Captain Preston and the soldiers to trial immediately. Many of the seamen who will be witnesses, says Adams, cannot afford to remain ashore for too many weeks.

Acting Governor Hutchinson, however, tries every legal maneuver possible to postpone the court hearings. Eventually he succeeds in deferring the trials of Preston and the soldiers until the August term of court. Because the court term continues until all cases are off the docket, this means that the redcoats probably will not face the jury until sometime in October. John Adams and Josiah Quincy, Jr., concur with Hutchinson; tempers are too inflamed at the moment to insure a fair trial.

Finding lawyers who will undertake the prosecution of the Britishers has proved a difficult job. The Patriots had looked forward to watching the Tories' finest attorneys try to prove that the King's soldiers murdered helpless citizens. But the Crown's attorney general, Jonathan Sewall, refused to get himself into such a predicament. He has left town. (Everyone says that he feared the mob might attack him.) Instead, the court has appointed two private lawyers, Robert Treat Paine and Samuel Quincy, to plead the Crown's case. Samuel is Josiah's older brother and is well known for his leanings toward Great Britain.

Oddly enough, Sam Adams is pleased that young Quincy and his own cousin John will defend the accused Britishers. He is anxious to have the men convicted, but he is even more anxious about the reputation of his beloved Boston. The Patriot leader knows well that there were rowdy acts on the night of March 5. It's very possible that testimony unfavorable to the town could emerge in the trials. If Crown lawyers had undertaken the defense, damaging disclosures would probably be made. But with John Adams and Josiah Quincy, Jr., as lawyers for the defense, Sam is certain that the activities of the citizenry will not appear in a bad light. Above all, the Patriot leader does not want the slightest whisper that there was any connivance by the town in the "horrid massacre."

Now in early April, Bostonians everywhere are talking about the prints from an engraving Paul Revere has made. In the press room of the *Boston Gazette,* editors Edes and Gill are finding it difficult to keep up with the demand for the pictures. Everyone wants to buy one of these prints, entitled: *The Bloody Massacre Perpetrated in King Street Boston on March 5th, 1770 by a party of the 29th Regt.*

The engraving is dominated by the facade and tower of the Town House, facing on King Street. Two other buildings converge on it from right and left. At the right is the Custom House, which Revere has labeled "Butcher's Hall." In the foreground on the right are seven British soldiers firing into a peaceful crowd of civilians, none of whom carries a rock or cudgel. Three victims of the gunfire lie on the ground; one is being carried away. Behind the soldiers Captain Preston is shown with sword upraised to order the firing. Below the scene is inscribed the following verse:

> Should venal Courts the scandal of the Land
> Snatch the relentless Villain from her Hand
> Keen Execrations on this Plate inscrib'd
> Shall reach a Judge that never can be brib'd

The first prints revealed the Town House clock hands pointing to 8 P.M. But after someone called this to Revere's attention, the silversmith doctored his engraving. Now the pictures show the time as 10:25, an hour more nearly correct.

However, there are still several inaccuracies in the scene—the peaceful civilians without weapons, the redcoats firing in a single volley rather than in ragged succession. Revere had no intention of making his engraving a precise representation of what happened on that tragic night. Rather it is a piece of propaganda and has been applauded by those Patriots who want to portray Boston as a tranquil town invaded by murderous soldiers. Many townsmen cannot read; with this picture before them, such people are convinced that the soldiers fired in cold blood on an innocent crowd.

Ever since leaving Boston on March 10, the two British regiments have been uncomfortably jammed into the barracks on Castle Island. Complaints from the soldiers are many. In mid-May, General Gage becomes convinced that it is not necessary to quarter so many men here. He writes Lieutenant Colonel Dalrymple to order one regiment sent south. Because Boston is so antagonistic toward the 29th Regiment, he suggests that it should be the one to leave. On May 17, the men are ferried over to Dorchester Neck and

commence their march to Providence, Rhode Island. The town celebrates the regiment's departure with bonfires and bell ringing.

Press reaction to the massacre has been varied. A South Carolina newspaper copied the style of the *Boston Gazette* and bordered the story with heavy black rules. Philadelphia reported the encounter as the "Bloody Massacre." But in New York City, where the Patriots are active in their protests also, the newspapers published objective accounts, never once referring to the incident as a "massacre."

Meanwhile, Sam Adams is highly suspicious of the reports being sent to London by Acting Governor

Hutchinson and the customs commissioners. Early in July, Sam learns that Benjamin Franklin, in London, has become the agent for the province, and the Patriot pens a letter immediately. He writes that he is pleased to learn that the *Short Narrative,* endorsed by town meeting, is "establishing the truth in the minds of honest men." But he's alarmed that Parliament may be swayed by "garbled reports" sent to London by the Crown officials.

Reaction to a possible bad press abroad is of genuine concern to the Patriots. At the town meeting of July 10, Sam Adams suggests that a report be prepared summarizing the "true state" of Boston since the night of March 5. A new committee is named to undertake the writing—a committee that includes Dr. Warren and Sam himself. The pamphlet, to be entitled *Additional Observations to a Short Narrative of the Horrid Massacre in Boston,* will be sent to those officials in England who may have been influenced by Hutchinson's accounts.

Late in July, some English newspapers reach Boston that disclose what Captain Preston has reported to Parliament. The Patriots are infuriated to read in the *Boston Gazette* what the captain has written:

> So bitter and inveterate are many of the Malcontents here that they are industriously using every Method

to fish out Evidence to prove it was a concerted Scheme to murder the Inhabitants. . . . I am though perfectly innocent, under most unhappy circumstances, having nothing in Reason to expect but the Loss of Life in a very ignominious manner, without the Interposition of His Majesty's Royal Goodness.

A committee is organized to visit Preston in jail and ask him for an explanation. The Britisher protests that what he wrote differed greatly from what has been reprinted. The Patriots resent what they consider an obvious falsehood.

During August, the town is filled with rumors. It's whispered that a mob is planning to snatch Captain Preston and the eight soldiers from jail for a probable lynching. Acting Governor Hutchinson tries to allay fears by saying that most Patriots discount such stories. They have told him that "whatever danger there may be after the trial, it would be the height of madness to think of any such thing before." Nevertheless Hutchinson asks Sheriff Stephen Greenleaf to take the keys from the jail keeper each night. If a mob should break in and demand entrance to the cells, the jailer could not deliver the keys. There's also a story making the rounds that even if the Britishers are found guilty, Hutchinson will pardon them.

Meanwhile, John Adams spends the summer

months preparing the case for the defense. Meticulously he searches his law books for statutes and precedents relating to the forthcoming trials. He goes over the rules that apply to homicide, seeking to learn the difference between justifiable homicide and that which is felonious. Day after day he walks through King Street, stepping off the distance between Murray's Barracks and the Custom House. And sometimes at night he returns to observe how the shadows fall at the hour of the massacre. Copious notes are recorded in his little black book.

Wherever he goes, the lawyer senses a rising tide of hostility toward himself. There are whistles and catcalls; mud is tossed at him in the streets. He is taunted by cries of "Who buys lobsters, John Adams?" Such incidents only serve to harden his resolve that the men in jail must receive a fair trial. One evening he returns home to find that two bricks have been thrown through a window of his house. His wife, Abigail, treats the matter lightly—it was only some rowdy youngsters, she says.

Nevertheless Abigail is seriously concerned about her husband. She seeks out their minister, Dr. Cooper of the Brattle Street Church, and asks him if he feels John's life is in danger. The minister is very reassuring. If the trials had been held immediately after the massacre, he says, there would have been cause to worry. But tempers have cooled. The citizens are more reasonable now. There's really no need for anxiety about her husband's safety.

As October approaches, John and Josiah Quincy, Jr., scour the town to find defense witnesses for the coming trials. The lawyers realize that some ninety-four persons have already sworn out depositions against the redcoats; many of them will be ready to testify if the prosecution chooses to call them.

Daily, Adams and Quincy meet with Robert Auchmuty to plan the strategy for their court sessions. The lawyers agree that an impartial jury must be impaneled. All England, perhaps all Europe, as well as all the colonies will be following these trials. If a verdict of acquittal can be secured—and it will be, declares Adams—then all the world will recognize that Boston is not ruled by hysteria and revenge. Instead, the citizens will have demonstrated their respect for law and justice.

Quincy and Auchmuty are not so confident of the verdict as is the fearless John Adams. They cannot help but wonder what the more vengeful citizens may be plotting if the redcoats are declared "Not guilty."

rex versus preston

october 24 – 30, 1770

The eight British privates, jailed immediately after the massacre on March 5, have become more and more irritable through the long summer months. Why should they be tried separately from their captain? they ask each other—even though they are well aware that enlisted men and officers are never on trial in the same court-martial. Nevertheless on October 21, Hugh White, James Hartegan, and Matthew Killroy draft an appeal to the Court. Their petition reads:

> We poor distressed prisoners beg that ye would be so good as to let us have our trial at the same time with our Captain, for we did our Captain's orders, and if we

do not obey his command should have been confined
and shot for not doing it. We only desire to open the
truths before our Captain's face for it is very hard that
he, being a gentleman, should have more chance for
to save his life than we poor men that is obliged to
obey his command.

The court promptly denies the appeal.

Now, on October 24, the trial of *Rex versus Preston*
is listed on the docket. Early this morning, defense
lawyers John Adams, Robert Auchmuty, and Josiah
Quincy, Jr., hurry over to the new Court House on
Queen Street. The case will be tried in the second-
floor courtroom, a spacious chamber with a fireplace at
one end. Before the fireplace is the bench—a long
table that accommodates the four-judge court. In front
of the bench are counsel tables, the clerk's desk, and
the jury box. Nearby is a small compartment where the
prisoner will be confined.

The defense lawyers seat themselves at their counsel
table and spread out their books and papers. Within a
few minutes the prosecution attorneys arrive. John
Adams peers at his opposition. Robert Treat Paine,
now solicitor general, has long been a legal rival. He's
well educated and understands law thoroughly, but he
can be overbearing at times. Samuel Quincy may not
be as brilliant as his younger brother, Josiah, but

Adams knows that Sam has a good mind and is capable of building a strong case.

The four judges—Justices Benjamin Lynde, John Cushing, Peter Oliver, and Edmund Trowbridge— sweep into the courtroom, awesome in their long red robes and flowing white wigs. (It's traditional that red is worn for murder trials.) Under heavy guard, Captain Preston is escorted to the prisoner's box. He looks wan from his long months in jail. Clerk of the Court Samuel Winthrop takes his place, and the room fills quickly with spectators.

Promptly at 8 A.M., court opens. The indictment is read; the prisoner asserts that his plea is "Not guilty." Jurors are called. John Adams, intent on achieving an impartial jury, challenges many of them. Several hours pass before the legal skirmishing is resolved and twelve men are seated in the jury box.

Samuel Quincy now rises to open for the Crown, and the trial begins. Quincy gives a detailed statement of what the prosecution intends to prove, and calls as his first witness Edward Garrick, the young apprentice to the wigmaker. Garrick describes his scuffle with sentry Private White and says that he had seen two groups of soldiers carrying swords before Captain Preston arrived on the scene.

The second Crown witness, Thomas Marshall, also

testifies that he saw those same soldiers, that they were shouting, "Fire!" and, "Let them come, by heaven!" When Peter Cunningham takes the stand, he swears that he heard Preston give the command to prime and load. William Wyare quotes the British captain as saying, "Damn your bloods, fire, be the consequence what it will!" The next four witnesses testify to having heard Preston shout those identical words.

By 5 P.M. the prosecution is still not finished—and the defense lawyers have not yet begun. Though a criminal trial in the Massachusetts Court has never lasted more than one day, it is obvious that this one will continue at least two or three. The judges and lawyers hold a hurried conference. It's agreed that the prosecution and the defense will each name a keeper, and that these two will be locked up with the jurors in the jail keeper's house nearby. Bedding, food, and "spirits" will be supplied.

When the trial resumes Thursday morning, October 25, more prosecution witnesses testify that they heard Preston order the shooting. But they also point out that the crowd's violence, the continual taunts from the bystanders, helped provoke the tragedy.

Crown lawyer Quincy now calls Daniel Calef to the stand. Calef emphasizes that he "heard the officer who stood on the right in a line with the soldiers give the word 'Fire' twice." He then describes Captain Preston: "I looked the officer in the face when he gave the word. He had on a red coat, yellow jacket, and silver-laced hat. . . . The prisoner is the officer I mean. I saw his face plain, the moon shone on it. I am sure of the man though I have not seen him since before yesterday when he came into Court. . . . I knew him instantly."

John Adams steals a glance at Josiah Quincy, Jr. If the jurors believe what Calef has stated, their only possible verdict will be "Guilty." This must not happen!

The next witnesses for the Crown can give only hearsay evidence. They all describe Acting Governor Hutchinson's angry interview with Captain Preston after the shooting—that Preston stated he had "to save his sentry," that he was forced "to save his own men." None heard the order to fire. Adams finds this encouraging for the defense, though privately he questions the Crown strategy. Good legal practice dictates that an attorney should always close with his strongest witness. Certainly Paine and Quincy have not followed this course.

Fifteen persons have been called to testify today. Now Samuel Quincy quickly sums up the testimony and closes with a quotation from the English jurist Sir

Edward Coke, which advises the jury that even if a felonious act is committed without thought, "the law implieth malice." The Crown rests.

John Adams arises and makes his opening statement for the defense. Because it is getting late in the afternoon, he calls only three witnesses: William Jackson, Benjamin Davis, Sr., and Edward Hill. Hill's testimony is by far the most pertinent. He recounts having seen Captain Preston after the firing push up a soldier's musket and say: "Fire no more. You have done mischief enough." After Hill finishes, the court is adjourned.

On the third day of the trial, John Adams calls twenty-two witnesses. From the testimony of the men who take the stand, the defense lawyer re-creates the scene in King Street on the night of March 5—a scene of mass confusion, noise, and threats. Joseph Edwards testifies that it was the corporal who gave the order to prime and load, *not* Preston. Joseph Hilyer states that "the soldiers seemed to act pure nature . . . I mean they acted and fired by themselves."

Merchant Richard Palmes recounts in detail how he first tried to make peace at Murray's Barracks, then hurried over to King Street to confront Captain Preston. He found the captain standing in front of his men. At the moment the command "Fire!" was heard,

Palmes says, he was conversing with the officer face to face. There was no way, asserts the witness, that Preston could have given the order.

Under oath Thomas Handasyd Peck, a fur exporter, recalls having asked Captain Preston after the shooting, "What have you done?" Preston, says Peck, answered: "Sir, it was none of my doings, the soldiers fired of their own accord. I was in the street and might have been shot."

Up to this moment in the trial, both prosecution and defense witnesses have testified only about what happened in King Street. Neither side has introduced evidence of earlier threats from soldiers or citizens. Now John Gillespie takes the stand. Questioned by Josiah Quincy, Jr., Gillespie states that he saw a gang of townspeople coming out of the South End at about 7 P.M. They were all armed with swords, clubs, and sticks. And, he adds, this was two hours before the shooting began.

John Adams is horrified. He bounds to his feet and asks the court for a brief adjournment. Taking Quincy by the elbow, Adams hustles the younger lawyer into an adjoining room. Does Quincy care nothing about the reputation of the town? Adams asks. By such questioning he can do great harm to the cause of liberty. Furthermore, the defense lawyer is not to elicit any further evidence that will tend "to show that the expulsion of the troops from Boston was a plan concerted among the inhabitants." Adams warns that if Quincy persists he will withdraw from the case. The younger lawyer promises to restrain himself.

After court has adjourned, Captain Preston and several of his friends accost John Adams: why was Mr. Quincy stopped in his skillful examination of John Gillespie? Is it possible that Adams is abandoning the British officer? The lawyer's eyes blaze with anger. Indeed he is not abandoning Preston, Adams retorts. But they must all remember that he has accepted this case only because he believes any accused person must have full benefit of the law. He proposes to conduct the trial in an impartial manner—or not at all.

When court reconvenes on Saturday morning, the defense rests. As is customary, the two defense lawyers will now give their closing arguments. John Adams rises and begins quoting from the great English lawmaker Sir William Blackstone: "Self-defense is the primary canon of the law of nature." In addition, says Adams, Blackstone asserts that if a man is assaulted and retreats, but can retreat no further, then it is permissible for him to kill his assailant to save his own life.

Point by point, the defense lawyer begins refuting

the Crown's evidence. On the question of conflicts in testimony, he says, "Man is a social creature. His passion and imagination are contagious. The circumstances had a tendency to move all passions. They had had a tendency to produce gloom and melancholy in all our minds. This may account for the variation in the testimony of honest men."

Adams now takes up Preston's side of the case. With great forensic skill he attempts to establish the innocence of the British captain. The defense's strongest evidence comes from Richard Palmes, whom Adams describes as "an inhabitant of the town, therefore not prejudiced in favor of soldiers." The jurors are reminded that Preston, although he knew the guns were loaded with ball, took his stance in front of the soldiers. Certainly, Adams postulates, "self-preservation would have made the captain alter his place at firing." With this dramatic statement, the lawyer ends his argument.

Senior counsel Robert Auchmuty comes forward and addresses the jurors, covering much the same legal ground as Adams. It is 4:30 P.M. when he finishes speaking. The court is adjourned; the jury will be locked up for the weekend.

On Monday, October 29, when the trial resumes, Robert Treat Paine gives his final argument for the

Crown. He does admit that there is "some little confusion in the evidence." The lawyer's voice is so low it's almost impossible to hear what he is saying.

Following the usual tradition, the judges now charge the jury. Justice Trowbridge gives a calm legal analysis of the case. First, he says, it must be established whether the crowd was an unlawful assembly. Next, did Captain Preston order the loading? "If it remains only doubtful in your minds whether he did order the loading or not," the judge continues, "you can't charge him with doing it." Further, did Preston actually give the command to fire?

Trowbridge reminds the jurors there has been much conflicting testimony. "If you are satisfied," he concludes, "that the sentinel was insulted and assaulted, and that Captain Preston and his party went to assist him, it was doubtless excusable homicide, if not justifiable. Self-defense is a law of nature, that every one of us has a right to, and may stand in need of."

Justice Trowbridge's statements are so methodical that the three remaining judges can add little to what has already been said; they all agree that "the principal question is whether the prisoner gave the order." It is now 5 P.M., and the jurors retire.

The next morning, Tuesday, October 30, when court reconvenes, foreman Joseph Mayo of Roxbury announces that the jury has reached a decision. The verdict is "Not guilty." A broad smile spreads across John Adams' face. Now all the world will know that law and justice are upheld by the town of Boston!

Highly pleased with his acquittal, Captain Preston writes to General Gage: "The counsel for the Crown, or rather the town, were poor and managed badly; my counsel on the contrary were men of parts and exerted themselves with great spirit and cleverness."

However, a new hazard threatens the captain. Relatives of "the murdered men" circulate stories that they will sue Preston for damages. Hastily he moves to the barracks at Castle William and applies for immediate passage back to England.

Meanwhile, the trial of the eight soldiers is set for Tuesday, November 27. John Adams wishes it could be sooner. Though Captain Preston's acquittal will probably make the coming trial easier, the defense lawyer is by no means certain of the outcome.

soldiers on trial

november 27 – december 5, 1770

The courtroom on Queen Street is filling rapidly with spectators on this Tuesday morning, November 27. Outside, a driving snow makes walking difficult. But no one wants to miss what will be, it is believed, "the greatest show ever staged in Boston."

Now seated at the counsel table are John Adams and Josiah Quincy, Jr. With them to assist in the defense of the soldiers is a young lawyer, Sampson Salter Blowers, who has been employed by friends of Captain Preston to help find witnesses and take affidavits. As in the previous trial, Robert Treat Paine and Samuel Quincy will represent the Crown.

Precisely at 8 A.M., the four justices—Edmund Trowbridge, Peter Oliver, John Cushing, and Benjamin Lynde—enter, looking regal in their scarlet robes and white wigs. Under guard the eight soldiers are led to the bar, their pale, expressionless faces in stark contrast to the stiff red coats they are wearing. They stand with their backs to the spectators as Clerk Samuel Winthrop reads the indictment:

"William Wemms, James Hartegan, William McCauley, Hugh White, Matthew Killroy, William Warren, John Carroll, and Hugh Montgomery not having the fear of God before their eyes, but being moved and seduced by the instigation of the devil and their own wicked hearts, did on the fifth day of this instant March, with force and arms, feloniously, willfully, and of their malice aforethought. . . ."

Specifically, the prisoners are charged as "principals and accessories" in the murder of five civilians. One by one the soldiers answer, "Not guilty"; Clerk Winthrop replies with the traditional response: "God send you a good deliverance!"

Jurymen now come forward to be challenged by the prisoners and their counsel. Again John Adams believes that it is of utmost importance to secure an impartial jury. Thirty men are disqualified before the specified twelve are sworn and take their places in the

box. They are all from surrounding towns—Dedham, Braintree, Roxbury, Milton, Stoughton, and Hingham. Not one resides in Boston.

Clerk Winthrop arises. "Prisoners, hold up your hands." Turning toward the jurors, he advises: "Good men and true, stand together and hearken to your evidence." The trial is thus formally begun.

Samuel Quincy opens for the Crown. "May it please your Honors, and you Gentlemen of the Jury," he says, "the cause is solemn and important; no less than whether eight of your fellow subjects shall live or die! A cause grounded on the most melancholy event that has yet taken place on the continent of America, and perhaps the greatest that has yet come before a tribunal of justice, in this part of the British dominions. . . . We are bound, not only by the natural obligations toward God and man, but also by oath, to examine into the evidence of fact without *partiality* or *prejudice;* I need not therefore caution you of your duty in this respect. . . ."

As Prosecutor Quincy begins calling his witnesses for questioning, there's a stir in the courtroom; necks are craned. Six men take the stand to tell their stories. All testify to the presence of off-duty soldiers armed with cutlasses who raced through the streets on that fatal night, assaulting citizens.

On Wednesday, eighteen more witnesses are called by the Crown. One, Samuel Hemmingway, a coachman for Sheriff Greenleaf, describes an evening prior to March 5, when he was with Matthew Killroy and heard him say that "he would never miss an opportunity, when he had one, to fire on the inhabitants, and that he had wanted to have an opportunity ever since he landed." Further, continues Hemmingway, "I said he was a fool for talking so. He said he did not care."

The Crown attempts to prove that there was little badgering of the soldiers as they stood in front of the Custom House. Nathaniel Fosdick, a hatter, is questioned about the people gathered in King Street. "Did you see any insults offered the soldiers?" prosecution lawyer Quincy asks. "No, none at all," asserts Fosdick.

Barber Benjamin Burdick relates a short conversation with Hugh Montgomery, describing him as "the prisoner who is bald on the head." Burdick says he asked Montgomery if the soldiers were going to fire; the redcoat replied, "Yes, by the Eternal God," and pushed at Burdick with his bayonet.

As testimony continues, the prosecution re-creates the scene on the night of March 5—the soldiers in an ugly mood, all of them looking for trouble with the townspeople. No witness remembers anything having been thrown at the redcoats; nor was there a hostile mob at the Custom House. But almost every witness recalls that Killroy and Montgomery fired into the crowd.

It is Thursday morning before Samuel Quincy closes evidence for the Crown. He then turns to the jury and says that in the view of the prosecution, there was no justification for the shots that killed five Boston civilians. After carefully reviewing the testimony of each witness, Quincy sums up: "The laws of society, gentlemen, lay a restraint on the passions of men, that no man shall be the avenger of his own cause. . . . If a man might at any time execute his own revenge, there would be an end of laws. . . . The facts against the prisoners at the bar are fully proved, and until something turns up to remove from your minds, the force of that evidence, you must pronounce them *Guilty!*"

Samuel Quincy is hardly seated before his younger brother, Josiah, is on his feet. John Adams watches his associate with a wary eye. The two have gone over the evidence with meticulous care; together they have devised a sound plan of strategy. Now, if only Josiah will keep his head and not be carried away by emotion.

"May it please your Honors, and you Gentlemen of the Jury," Josiah begins, "the prisoners at the bar stand indicted for the murder of five of His Majesty's liege subjects, as set forth in the several indictments.

. . . Permit me, gentlemen, to remind you of the importance of their trial as it relates to the prisoners. It is for their lives! . . . An opinion has been entertained by many among us, that the life of a *soldier* was of very little value; of much less value than others of the community. The law, gentlemen, knows no such distinction; the life of a soldier is viewed by the equal eye of the law, as estimable as the life of any other citizen."

The defense lawyer now launches into a lengthy description of the relationship of Massachusetts Bay with England. It was, he says, Parliament's encroachment on the liberties of Boston citizens that aroused the town to protect their rights. When the soldiers arrived in the autumn of 1768, "no room was left for cordiality and friendship. Discontent was seated on almost every brow. Instead of that hospitality which the soldier thought himself entitled to, scorn, contempt, and silent murmurs were his reception."

Josiah, in speaking of the night of March 5, admits that parties of soldiers were out to quarrel with townspeople, but this, he emphasizes, has no bearing on the encounter in front of the Custom House. The jurors' only concern must be whether Preston's soldiers were justified in the firing of their guns. In conclusion, he says:

"Gentlemen, great pains have been taken by different men, with different views, to involve the character, the conduct, and the reputation of the town of Boston in the present issue. Boston and its inhabitants have no more to do with this cause than you, or any other members of the community.

"You are therefore, by no means to blend together two things, so essentially different, as the guilt or innocence of this town and the prisoners. The inhabitants of Boston, by no rules of law, justice, or common sense, can be supposed answerable for the unjustifiable conduct of a few individuals hastily assembled in the streets. Every populous city, in like circumstances, would be liable to similar commotions, if not worse. . . . Who can, who will, unnecessarily interest himself to justify the rude behavior of a mixed and ungovernable multitude? May I not appeal to you, and all who have heard this trial thus far, that things already wear a different aspect from what we have been heretofore taught to expect?"

The jury is visibly stirred by Josiah's eloquence. He seems to have achieved his purpose of persuading the jurors to discard preconceived ideas and to consider the facts brought out by the defense. After reviewing in minute detail the Crown evidence, the lawyer begins calling up his witnesses. Fifteen men testify before court is adjourned at 5 P.M.

All day Friday and Saturday the court hears defense witnesses; a total of forty persons testify during these two days. Most tell a story similar to that of Daniel Cornwall, who recounts having found a large crowd in front of the Custom House. "I saw them throwing oyster shells and snowballs at the sentry at the Custom House door," he says. "Some were hallooing out, 'Let us burn the sentry box, let us heave it overboard,' but they did neither. . . . Just before the soldiers fired, I heard the people say, 'Damn you, fire, you bloody backs.'"

It is 5 P.M. Saturday afternoon when the last witness leaves the stand. He is Dr. John Jeffries, who was with Patrick Carr when he died. The physician has related a conversation with Carr, in which the victim said "he really thought they did fire to defend themselves, that he did not blame the man, whoever he was, that shot him."

Now the court rises. The jurors are led out to be confined in the jail keeper's house for the weekend.

On Monday morning at 9 A.M., the trial reopens to hear Josiah Quincy, Jr., sum up for the defense. He is on his feet for more than an hour, pointing out pertinent evidence. In conclusion, he says: "I cannot close this cause better than by desiring you to consider well the genius and spirit of the law, and to govern

yourselves by this great standard of truth. . . ."
Josiah now leans toward the jury box and, in a voice
that's low and almost hypnotic in quality, adds: "May
the blessing of those, who were in jeopardy of life,
come upon you—may the blessing of him who is 'not
faulty to die,' descend and rest upon you and your
posterity."

The courtroom is silent as Quincy returns to the
counsel table. Spectators and jurors alike are dazed by
the dramatic rhetoric that the lawyer has displayed.

John Adams arises to make the closing remarks.
"May it please your Honors, and you, Gentlemen of
the Jury," he says, "I am for the prisoners at the bar
and shall apologize for it only in the words of the
Marquis Beccaria, 'If I can but be the instrument of
preserving one life, his blessing and tears of transport
shall be a sufficient consolation to me, for the contempt
of all mankind.' "

At these words both jurors and spectators turn
toward the prisoners. The soldiers, who have sat
almost motionless through the long days of testimony,
shift in their seats and exchange glances. Is it possible
that the jury may show some mercy after all?

"As the prisoners stand before you for their lives,"
Adams continues, "it may be proper to recollect with
what temper the law requires that we should proceed

to this trial. . . . The spirit of the law upon such occasions, is conformable to humanity, to common sense and feeling; . . . it is all benignity and candor."

Adams now instructs the jury in the three kinds of homicide: justifiable, excusable, and felonious. "Felonious homicide," he explains, "is subdivided into two branches; the first is murder, which is killing with malice aforethought; the second is manslaughter, which is killing a man on a sudden provocation. . . . God Almighty, whose laws we cannot alter, has planted in every man the quality of self-defense, the first and strongest principle of our nature."

The jurors nod agreement. Adams steps nearer the box and looks every man in the eye before speaking. "Place yourselves in the situation of Killroy or the sentry . . . with all the bells ringing, the people shouting, huzzahing, and making the mob whistle, as they call it, which when a boy makes it in the street is no formidable thing, but when made by a multitude, is a most hideous shriek, almost as terrible as an Indian yell; the people crying 'Kill them! Knock them over!', heaving snowballs, oyster shells, clubs, white birch sticks three and a half inches in diameter.

"Consider yourselves, in this situation, and then judge, whether a reasonable man, in the soldiers' situation, would not have concluded they were going to kill him. . . . The law considers a man capable of bearing anything and everything but blows. . . . Every snowball, oyster shell, cake of ice or bit of cinder thrown that night at the sentinel and the party of soldiers was an assault upon them whether it hit any of them or not."

Adams now begins quoting foremost English barristers on the law, and translates their technical language into terms that every juror can understand. Glancing at the wall clock, the lawyer notes that it is nearly 5 P.M. In closing, he says: "I desire not to advance anything of my own. I choose to lay down rules of law from authorities that cannot be disputed." Court is adjourned.

When the trial resumes Tuesday morning, Adams proceeds to examine the defense testimony. Without emotion he states the facts, point by point. Before closing, he wants to show that it was not the town that was involved in the tragedy, but only a small segment of the people.

"We have been entertained," he says, "with a great variety of phrases, to avoid calling this sort of people a mob. The plain English is, gentlemen, it was most probably a motley rabble. . . . And why we should scruple to call such a set of people a mob, I can't conceive, unless the name is too respectable for them.

The sun is not about to stand still or go out because there was a mob in Boston the fifth of March that attacked a party of soldiers. Such things are not new in the world, nor in the British dominions, though they are, comparatively, rarities and novelties in this town."

Several more hours are consumed by Adams' examination of the Crown testimony. In conclusion, he states: "Facts are stubborn things and whatever may be our wish, our inclinations, or the dictates of our passions, they cannot alter the state of facts and evidence. . . . To your candor and justice I submit the prisoners and their cause."

As lawyer Adams returns to his seat, he glances at the spectators. Yes, cousin Sam is still there taking copious notes, just as he has been throughout the trial. What does Sam propose to do? John wonders.

Robert Treat Paine now comes forward to close for the Crown. He reminds the jury that if it finds the soldiers were unlawfully assembled, they must all be guilty, "for it has been abundantly proved to you by the numerous authorities produced by the counsel for the prisoners, that every individual of an unlawful assembly is answerable for the doings of the rest." By 5:30 P.M., the jurors are weary, the audience restless. Court is adjourned.

On Wednesday morning, December 5, spectators

arrive long before the trial begins at 8 A.M. Everyone knows that today the case will go to the jury; no one wants to miss the verdict. After Paine finishes his summation, the four judges instruct the jurors, and the twelve men file out to consider the evidence.

An hour passes, then another. John Adams becomes more and more anxious. He had expected a speedy verdict. What can be taking so long? If the soldiers are found guilty of manslaughter, Adams and Quincy have already decided to ask for "benefit of clergy." This disposition is based on an ancient English law that formerly applied only to ministers, who could demand trial by an ecclesiastical court, which could not inflict the death penalty. Today in Massachusetts Bay, "benefit of clergy" extends to all who can read and write. If granted, the prisoner is branded on the thumb and discharged.

After two and a half hours, the jurors return to their box. There is complete silence in the courtroom as the foreman reads the decision:

> William Wemms, James Hartegan, William McCauley, Hugh White, William Warren and John Carroll: NOT GUILTY. Matthew Killroy and Hugh Montgomery, not guilty of murder, but GUILTY OF MANSLAUGHTER.

John Adams springs up quickly and asks for benefit

of clergy for Killroy and Montgomery. The justices grant it. The six freed soldiers leave the courtroom while the branding iron is heated over the open fire. Killroy and Montgomery are burned on the thumb. The trial is over.

Afterwards, the redcoats seek out Adams and Quincy to offer their thanks—they owe the two lawyers their lives, they say. And where should they go now in order to be safe? Adams suggests that the soldiers proceed out to Castle William immediately, where they will be under Crown protection.

And what about Mr. Adams and Mr. Quincy? the soldiers ask. Are they in any danger?

With a weary smile John Adams answers, "Gentlemen, remember that you have been acquitted by a jury of our countrymen. And Boston is our home!"

hostility subsides

december 1770 – january 1771

As the year 1770 fades into 1771, Boston is noticeably quieter than it has been for many months. Ironically enough, it was on the very day of the massacre that Lord John North, the King's new First Minister, introduced in Parliament a motion to repeal the Townshend Acts—all the obnoxious taxes that had infuriated the colonists, except for the tax on tea.

Now that most imports from England are no longer taxed, Boston stores are filled with a tempting array of figured wallpapers and house paints; mirrors and glass sconces ("for the Mantelpiece"); lusterware and Scottish carpets; gloves, woolens, satins, and brocades.

Merchants are doing more business than they have for years. Leading importers say that it's time to stop quarreling with England about taxation and colonial rights.

The customs commissioners now report to Acting Governor Hutchinson that they have "no complaints of insults or any sort of molestation." His Majesty's 14th Regiment is still quartered out at Castle William, but Lieutenant Colonel Dalrymple plans to have it join the 29th in New Jersey very soon. He intends to send the troops by sea; the commander is fearful that if they march by land there will be too many deserters.

Sam Adams and his Patriot friends Dr. Warren, Paul Revere, and Will Molineux continue to hold conferences for the express purpose of keeping the cause of liberty alive. In January, Sam launches a series of five articles in the *Boston Gazette,* signed with the pen name "Vindex." Point by point he refutes the defense testimony and hints that witnesses told only half of what they knew. He had hoped for a verdict of "Guilty" for Captain Preston and the soldiers; it would have had great propaganda value for the Patriots. Nevertheless, he is pleased that his cousin John and Josiah Quincy, Jr., did not allow the town's reputation to be tarnished.

In addition, Sam manages to persuade the authori-

ties that March 5 should be a "day of mourning"—
that it should become an annual occasion with appropriate oratory. Adams wants to keep the memory of
the "horrible massacre" very much alive for the local
citizenry.

Meanwhile, John Adams is finding himself in a
difficult position. Some of the Patriots are insinuating
that John has turned against their cause. The Tories
believe that the lawyer is now one of them despite the
fact that Adams has never given them any reason to
think so. Though the personal risk was great, he has
followed the oath of his profession in defending nine
innocent men. His only concern had been justice, and
he is satisfied that justice has been done. To his diary
he confides:

> The Part I took in Defence of Captn. Preston and the
> Soldiers, procured me Anxiety, and Obloquy enough.
> It was, however, one of the most gallant, generous,
> manly and disinterested Actions of my whole Life, and
> one of the best pieces of Service I ever rendered my
> Country. Judgment of Death against these Soldiers
> would have been as foul a Stain upon this Country as
> the Executions of the Quakers or Witches, anciently.
> As the Evidence was, the Verdict of the Jury was
> exactly right.

Despite the apparent calmness in this January of

1771, the events of last March have affected Bostonians in their growing discontent with England. They now know how dangerous uncontrolled Royal authority can be. Unjust taxes and laws imposed by Parliament had provoked the unrest. This, in turn, brought the English redcoats to maintain obedience. The tragedy that followed has proved that there are fundamental differences between the Mother Country and the colonies—that irrational acts of stupidity can lead to disastrous consequences.

The massacre has made the possibility of revolution and independence seem less remote—perhaps, even necessary. However, Boston is still a part of the British Empire. Is it possible that now, with the soldiers gone, a lasting peace can be achieved?

bibliography

Adams, John. Diary and Autobiography. 4 vols. Edited by L. H. Butterfield. Cambridge, Mass.: Belknap Press, Harvard University Press, 1961.

The Adams Papers: Legal Papers of John Adams. L. K. Wroth and H. B. Zobel, editors. 3 vols. Cambridge, Mass.: Harvard University Press, 1965.

Adams, Randolph G. New Light on the Boston Massacre. Proceedings of the American Antiquarian Society, 1937. Vol. 47, pp. 259–354.

Andrews, Charles. The Colonial Background of the American Revolution. New Haven: Yale University Press, 1924.

Bacon, Edwin M. Rambles Around Old Boston. Boston: Little, Brown and Company, 1921.

Beach, Stewart. Samuel Adams: The Fateful Years, 1764–1776. New York: Dodd, Mead & Company, 1965.

Boston Looks Seaward: The Story of the Port, 1630–1940. Boston: Bruce Humphries, Inc., 1941.

Bowen, Catherine Drinker. John Adams and the American Revolution. Boston: Little, Brown and Company, 1950.

Bridenbaugh, Carl. Cities in Revolt: Urban Life in America, 1743–1776. New York: Alfred A. Knopf, Inc., 1955.

———. The Colonial Craftsman. New York: New York University Press, 1950.

Buckingham, Joseph T. Specimens of Newspaper Literature with Personal Memoirs, Anecdotes, and Reminiscences, vol. 1. Boston: Charles C. Little and James Brown, 1850.

Chamberlain, Allen. Beacon Hill. Boston: Houghton Mifflin Company, 1925.

Chidsey, Donald Barr. The Loyalists: The Story of Those Americans Who Fought Against Independence. New York: Crown Publishers, Inc., 1973.

Comstock, Sarah. Roads to the Revolution. New York: Macmillan Company, 1928.

Crawford, Mary Caroline. Old Boston Days and Ways. Boston: Little, Brown and Company, 1913.

———. Old Boston in Colonial Days. Boston: Page Company, 1908.

Dickerson, Oliver, editor. Boston Under Military Rule, 1768–1769, as Revealed in a Journal of the Times. Boston: Chapman and Grimes, 1936.

Dow, George Francis. Everyday Life in the Massachusetts Bay Colony. Boston: Society for the Preservation of New England Antiquities, 1935.

Drake, Samuel A. Old Boston Taverns. Boston: Cupples, Upham & Company, 1886.

———. Old Landmarks and Historic Personages of Boston. Boston: Little, Brown and Company, 1873.

———. Our Colonial Homes. Boston: Lee & Shepard, Publishers, 1894.

Fisher, Sydney George. The Struggle for American Independence, vol. 1. Philadelphia: J. B. Lippincott Company, 1908.

Forbes, Esther. The Boston Book. Boston: Houghton Mifflin Company, 1947.

————. Paul Revere and the World He Lived in. Boston: Houghton
   Mifflin Company, 1942.

Fritz, Jean. Cast for a Revolution, 1728–1814. Boston: Houghton
   Mifflin Company, 1972.

Gipson, Lawrence Henry. The Coming of the Revolution, 1763–1775.
   New York: Harper and Brothers, 1954.

Hansen, Harry. The Boston Massacre: An Episode of Dissent and
   Violence. New York: Hastings House, 1970.

Hosmer, James K. Samuel Adams. Boston: Houghton Mifflin,
   1885.

Jennings, John. Boston: Cradle of Liberty, 1630–1776. Garden City,
   N.Y. Doubleday and Company, 1947.

Jensen, Merrill. The Founding of a Nation. New York: Oxford
   University Press, 1968.

Kidder, Frederic. History of the Boston Massacre. Albany, N.Y.: J.
   Munsell, 1870.

Knollenberg, Bernhard. Origin of the American Revolution. New
   York: Macmillan Company, 1960.

Maier, Pauline. From Resistance to Revolution: Colonial Radicals and
   the Development of American Opposition to Britain, 1765–1776.
   New York: Alfred A. Knopf, Inc., 1972.

Mann, Albert W. Walks and Talks About Historic Boston. Boston:
   Mann Publishing Company, 1917.

Matthews, Albert. Captain Thomas Preston and the Boston Massacre.
   Publications of the Colonial Society of Massachusetts, vol. 7, 1905.

Miller, John C. Origins of the American Revolution. Boston: Little,
   Brown and Company, 1943.

————. Sam Adams: Pioneer in Propaganda. Boston: Little, Brown
   and Company, 1936.

Mott, Frank Luther. American Journalism: A History, 1690–1960.
   New York: Macmillan Company, 1962.

Schlesinger, Arthur M. The Birth of the Nation: A Portrait of the

American People on the Eve of Independence. New York: Alfred A. Knopf, Inc., 1968.

―――. The Colonial Merchants and the American Revolution, 1763–1776. New York: Columbia University Press, 1918.

―――. Prelude to Independence: The Newspaper War on Britain, 1764–1776. New York: Alfred A. Knopf, Inc., 1958.

Scudder, Horace Elisha. Boston Town. Boston: Houghton Mifflin Company, 1881.

A Short Narrative of the Horrid Massacre in Boston, . . . Boston: printed by order of the town on the press of Edes & Gill, 1770.

Smith, Page. John Adams. 2 vols. Garden City, N.Y.: Doubleday and Company, 1962.

Thwing, Annie Haven. Crooked and Narrow Streets of the Town of Boston. Boston: Marshall Jones Company, 1920.

Trial of the British Soldiers. Boston: Belcher and Armstrong, 1807.

Truax, Rhoda. The Doctors Warren of Boston. Boston: Houghton Mifflin Company, 1968.

Warden, G. B. Boston, 1689–1776. Boston: Little, Brown and Company, 1970.

Weston, George F., Jr. Boston Ways: High, By, and Folk. Boston: Beacon Press, 1957.

Zobel, Hiller B. The Boston Massacre. New York: W. W. Norton & Company, Inc., 1970.

Newspapers 1768–1770:
Boston Evening Post
Boston Gazette
Boston News-Letter
The Chronicle

index

About the Author

Mary Kay Phelan's career as a writer began in response to questions from her two young sons. When, after a trip to Washington, D.C., she could not find a book that satisfied their demands for more information about the White House, she wrote one herself. And she has continued to write books that bring American history vividly to life. Mrs. Phelan is the author of Four Days in Philadelphia— 1776, *which tells the story of the adoption of the Declaration of Independence;* Midnight Alarm: The Story of Paul Revere's Ride; The Story of the Great Chicago Fire, 1871; Mr. Lincoln's Inaugural Journey; The Story of the Boston Tea Party; The Burning of Washington: August 1814; Probing the Unknown: The Story of Dr. Florence Sabin; Martha Berry; *and three books in the Crowell Holiday series—*Mother's Day, The Fourth of July, *and* Election Day.

Born in Kansas, Mrs. Phelan was graduated from DePauw University in Indiana and received her master's degree in English from Northwestern University. She has worked as an advertising copywriter, and she and her husband are now involved in the production of historical films that are widely used in schools and libraries. The Phelans live in Davenport, Iowa, most of the year but enjoy their frequent travels in this country and in Europe.

About the Illustrator

A native of Minnesota, Allan Eitzen attended college and art schools in Minneapolis and Philadelphia. He interrupted his formal studies for on-the-job training with a religious publishing firm, and after several years returned to art school with an appreciation of the skills required in pictorial reproduction. Mr. Eitzen subsequently began a free-lance career; he particularly enjoys assignments that involve sketching trips.

Mr. Eitzen, his wife, and the youngest of their five children live in Barto, Pennsylvania, in an old home whose remodeling takes up much of the artist's spare time.